Praise for *Turn*

"Modernity gives an account of a world of already-made parts, a world of complete things, immobile in their frozen ontologies. A world where full descriptions are possible. In this fluid, enrapturing spell of a book, Brie Stoner stirs up a process philosophy of life in which boundaries are never still, bodies live only through other bodies, and the orphaned 'I' of colonial lore finds itself already orgasmically entangled in a vast movement that exceeds its isolation. What emerges from this textual lovemaking is a practical, down-to-earth paean to a cosmic intimacy, a prior generosity, that connects our relationships, our failures, and our most vulnerable moments of love and seeking to every rock, bump, and shadow in the world. No one and nothing is spared the reach of Brie's embrace."

—**Bayo Akomolafe**, PhD, author of *These Wilds Beyond Our Fences: Letters to My Daughter on Humanity's Search for Home*

"Brie Stoner tunes us to the most vastly embracing and most intimately touching energy of the universe, releasing afresh the ancient imagery of the cosmic Eros."

—**Catherine Keller**, George T. Cobb Professor of Constructive Theology, Drew University Theological School, and author of *Facing Apocalypse: Climate, Democracy, and Other Last Chances*

"There is so much wisdom in this book, alongside humor and an immense tenderness. Reading this, I was reminded that creativity is a form of divinity. It is cultivated through presence. It can be found while sitting in the sun for five minutes and eating an orange, as well as by creating an artwork. Stoner doesn't offer quick fixes for more creativity. She points readers toward deeper awareness and embodiment, in the service of a richer and more meaningful life. What a generous gift she has offered readers."

—**Lora Mathis**, visual artist and author of *The Snakes Came Back*

"Some books tell you how to be happy and successful in a pretty little box. Some books tell you how to escape the box and embark on a life-changing adventure. *Turned On* is one of the latter. It dares you to believe that the universe is about creativity and that you are a maker, an artist, a person capable of adding life to life and joy to joy."

—**Brian D. McLaren**, author of *Faith After Doubt* and *Life After Doom*

"In this playful, poetic book, philosopher and musician Brie Stoner distills the intoxicating essence of her own path to reclaiming the sacred feminine. Her words spill like song onto the page, mingling her brilliant mind and generous heart, offering us a luminous path to our birthright of creativity and connection."

—**Mirabai Starr**, author of *Wild Mercy* and *Ordinary Mysticism*

"*Faith. Creativity. Desire.* These powerful words are too often uttered with anthropocentric abstraction. In Stoner's fierce blend of memoir and rigorous research, they once again grow bodies, leaking past the sterility of human cognition and back into our divine overlap with the animate, appetitive earth."

—**Sophie Strand**, author of *The Flowering Wand* and *The Madonna Secret*

"Brie Stoner offers us a sensual cosmology. Her god is Eros—the foundational desire to create that brings forth life on all levels. For Stoner, Eros is the source of reality—and therefore the truest guideline to live a fully human life, which she invites us into with sparkling storytelling and a sensuality that never feels over the top."

—**Andreas Weber**, biologist and philosopher,
author of *Matter and Desire: An Erotic Ecology*

Turned On

TURNED ON

A Creative's Guide to Awakening Presence, Pleasure, and Possibility

BRIE STONER

Broadleaf Books
Minneapolis

TURNED ON
A Creative's Guide to Awakening Presence, Pleasure, and Possibility

29 28 27 26 25 24 1 2 3 4 5 6 7 8 9

Library of Congress Cataloging-in-Publication Data

Names: Stoner, Brie, author.
Title: Turned on : a creative's guide to awakening presence, pleasure, and possibility / Brie Stoner.
Description: Minneapolis : Broadleaf Books, [2025] | Includes bibliographical references.
Identifiers: LCCN 2024008576 | ISBN 9798889831624 (paperback) | ISBN 9798889831631 (ebook)
Subjects: LCSH: Stoner, Brie. | Self-realization. | Creative ability. | Pleasure. | Conduct of life.
Classification: LCC BJ1470 .S76 2025 | DDC 306.77—dc23/eng/20240604
LC record available at https://lccn.loc.gov/2024008576

Cover illustration by Izzy Spitz
Cover design by Izzy Spitz

Print ISBN: 979-8-8898-3162-4
eBook ISBN: 979-8-8898-3163-1

Contents

The Overture

> **noun/** *1. an orchestral piece at the beginning of an opera, suite, play, oration, or other extended composition. 2. an introduction to something more substantial. 3. an approach to someone with the aim of establishing a relationship.*
>
> —Oxford Languages

> *Art is the act of triggering deep memories of what it means to be fully human.*
>
> —David Whyte

If you and I were on a first date, I would probably wear my red dress. It has three-quarter-length sleeves, a wide-open décolletage, and it makes me feel confidently feminine, even if I always pair it with a pair of vintage leather '70s boots for a little rock-and-roll grit. While I can stand on a stage and perform in front of thousands of people, I'm a different creature when it comes to love, so I'd likely be shy, probably a little twitchy and awkward, but hopefully in a charming way. I'd wait to see what kind of questions you asked as a measure of what matters to you. And if you asked about my past, what shaped me, what animates my soul, I would tell you about my childhood in Spain, about my parents' devotion to art, and how that all served as a backdrop to my discovering my own desire to be a maker in this world. I would probably say it just like that actually. Which is fine. We are, after all, just getting to know each other.

But if one date turned to two, and the days bled together into weeks, the stories would begin coming out in greater detail and vibrancy. I would give them to you from time to time, as an offering of love, as a gift, as a way for you to climb into a moment in my life and see the world through my eyes.

These memories are not linear. They're glimpses of how desire moves me. I'd give them to you anyway, like a love-filled Post-it note on the bathroom mirror or a random text in the afternoon. A hushed offering lying in bed when the fury of passion gives way to contented stillness.

Each memory I give you, each note, is like one I reach for from the handful of Polaroids in a drawer that is me. Some are photographic in their clarity; some are impressionist images, colorful sketches quickly drawn, hinting at the shape of my becoming. But the one thing they have in common is that all of them orbit around the singular axis of my life, the one thing that has been core to my being from the beginning: making.

Here are a few I would give you, early on, Polaroids of moments that reveal the bloom of desire, of life, of love in my life . . . Eros ever seducing me from the comfort of the familiar into unknown, unimagined possibilities of *more*. At first, these stories may feel random. And then you realize that every memory, every story, is part of a larger one, and as I share them with you, they become part of our shared story, together. Because that's what Love does. Love is the thread that runs through everything, creating coherence out of every seemingly disparate moment in our lives, providing the heft and weft of the tapestries we weave. Love, what makes a *we* out of you and me.

* * *

Here is one memory.

The light streamed in sideways through the floor-to-ceiling windows in a studio in Madrid. After the smell of acrylic and oil paint, what struck me was always the light in this loft studio that was a weekly trap door to another world in the middle of the city. Ramiro, a renowned painter in his late seventies then, quietly ran the studio, living the final quarter of his life in service of shaping the creative capacity of children and young adults. The short, bald Spaniard frequently took out a handkerchief to dab at the edges of his mouth where saliva sometimes collected. His humble stature was dwarfed by the immense calm, absolute self-assurance, and quiet dignity of a man who, having faced the dragons of life, transformed them into beauty, into art.

After he ensured we had our paint palettes and brushes, he began the class, almost as though invoking religious ceremony. Ramiro, our high priest, hand mixing acrylic paint, walked around distributing the holy host in dazzling pigment form, followed by a quick ten-minute "mass." Sometimes he would talk about the still lives he set up, about line and movement and negative space. Sometimes he would talk about feeling, impression, and freedom from how things "ought" to be. But *always* he radiated warmth, presence, peace, and the grace-filled permission to move toward what *could* be.

After his talk, we—tiny parishioners—set to work, each of us industriously at our stations: the initial charcoal sketches followed by paint. Ramiro would walk behind us, correcting the posture of an arm here, asking a provoking question there, delighting in this child's work, untangling the stuck frustration of that other child. His warm register could be quietly heard, urging his eager students.

The timbre of the room would always settle into a quiet hum like one would find in a cathedral . . . with nothing but the soft hiss of a brush on paper, sounding like shuffling feet in line for communion. Or like the awed whisper of angels as they witnessed with wonder this human creative manifestation happen.

And there, in the corner, I stood. A little girl with dirty blond hair in a too-big blue painter's robe with the sleeves rolled up, staring down the infinity of potential with the intensity of a matador looking at a bull. My heart beating once, twice, three times . . . *make me, make me, make me.* Until at last, suddenly unfrozen, inspiration drove my movement. With assured finality, with confident intensity, with desire, my hand moved, daring unseen shapes to become real before me. Daring what hadn't been, to be.

* * *

Another Polaroid.

I'm a grown woman in a coffee shop in upstate New York, with a man, standing in line, absentmindedly watched the people ahead of us. I loved the feeling of his arms around me, leaning my back against his tall frame. When I took a step forward, he brushed my hair aside and kissed the back of my neck. It was a simple, small gesture . . . inconspicuous even. But there, where his lips had been a moment before, a trail of fire ignited and ran all the way down my spine, animating the most ancient of all instincts. One minute ago, I had been passively staring at nothing; the next moment I was on full alert and seemingly seared to a singular and all-encompassing purpose. Turning suddenly to face him, I saw that this innocent gesture of his was not entirely detached from this precise, hoped-for response. His arms still around me, he leaned back with an expression feigning complete ignorance, eyes twinkling . . . "Yes? Did you need something? May I help y—?" Turnabout was fair play. I returned the favor and silenced him with little regard for my rather passionate public display of affection and the eye-rolling around us. We couldn't care less, dissolving into laughter when the woman behind us cut ahead with an annoyed, "Oh, get a room already!"

* * *

A huddle of tiny ballerinas is crouched by the corner of a mirrored ballet studio, crushing amber resin into powder with their slippered feet, while others are stretching or getting their toe shoes ready. I'm on the floor warming up, the smallest dancer of the class. There are certain sounds and sensations you never forget from ballet . . . and this is one. The crunch always felt strangely satisfying as we pulverized the chunks down. As did banging new shoes against the ground or the burning away of the tips of the satin. All tips to help break the toe shoes in, all sounds that create the soundtrack of dancers changing, stretching, warming up. In this scene, Olga started us on pointe, and one of the girls showed up with cushions to place at the toe bed. Olga, trained in the Russian school of ballet, trained us likewise in the same philosophy of that school, and cushioning the toes—or any other shortcut way to minimize discomfort in the perpetual discomfort known as ballet—was not part of the program. "Cushioning is a great way for your toes to fall asleep and not feel," she said as she threw the cushions in the trash. A singular small, one-inch-diameter toe-tip to wooden floor. Human toes to ribbon-ensconced cast. Yes, it hurt. That was the only chain of contact allowed when in *relevé,* as tiny circular touch points where gravity served its function. Pain was part of the process, so we learned to befriend the ache of our muscles, the strain of our stretches, and yes, the pressure on the tips of our toes. There when you could truly feel everything, you were making impact. There where you could truly feel everything, you were moving art.

* * *

I caught my mom's gaze through the rearview mirror as she drove us to high school in our Dodge Intrepid. In just that one glance lived a question and an apology . . . and I could tell how worried she was, how guilty she felt. I quickly looked out the window so I didn't have to answer her gaze. We were moving *again*. Just when I was *finally* feeling like I had some semblance of a life with a group of amazing friends in Indiana, after having moved from Spain three years prior. I couldn't believe what I was hearing. Rage boiled in my blood alongside the powerlessness of not being able to do anything about it. Life ebbed out of my heart in a resigned hiss.

I don't want to go away. Not again.

Please, God, don't make me have to start all over again.

I repeated the pointless litany. My dad had already accepted the teaching position in Michigan. We were moving.

Moving through classes like a zombie, I told my friends I was on my period to allay their concerned looks, to avoid telling them the truth: I was going to lose them. I was leaving.

When the bell rang, I couldn't get on the bus fast enough. My anger began to rise once more, but just before reaching the defeated powerlessness again, I suddenly knew the one thing I *could* do. The *only* thing I could do.

Storming into the house, ignoring my parents and my brother arguing in the kitchen, I went straight for my dad's guitar, hauled it into my room, and locked the door. Now the fury moved along the fretboard repeating my litany . . . until it morphed into lyrics. Until my heartbreak became my first song.

Making Love

An Introduction

> *When I speak of the erotic, then, I speak of it as an assertion of the lifeforce of women; of that creative energy empowered, the knowledge and use of which we are now reclaiming in our language, our history, our dancing, our loving, our work, our lives.*
>
> —Audre Lorde

My entire life, I have been devoted to the creative act. If I had to peel back the inherited beliefs, narratives, religious meanderings, spiritual practices, and philosophical explorations into the purest expression of what constitutes the center of my experience, that one sentence feels like it comes closest to articulating the key in which I am singing the song of my life. Now, I would describe that creative act *as* Eros—the desire of life-force on its way to making more life. But it's taken me a long time to learn that what I had been taught to see as separate are really, in fact, all one thing in essence. A lake is certainly different from a river, or a puddle, or the ocean, but they are all water, after all. But when we are children, we are taught to see and understand the world by what differentiates, not by what binds.

My parents were Baptist missionaries to Spain, which is ironic to those who know that Spain is a deeply devout Catholic country. Despite the mission's evangelical focus on proselytizing, my parents dedicated themselves to serving the community through antidrug programs, a youth center, basketball tournaments, and care of AIDS patients, ostracized even in the hospitals in the 1980s.

We had no television, so my parents gifted my brother and me with books, books, and more books. We read constantly, and the strict theology I was ensconced in was paradoxically liberated through the magical worlds of the literature of Tolkien, Lewis, McDonald, and L'Engle. That liberation extended to the arts. My parents were great lovers of the Impressionists, so we traipsed through Europe to visit the studios of the greats and were exposed to every possible collection in any museum within driving distance. Picasso, Matisse, Cezanne. My father played classical guitar and led worship for the small church we were part of. My earliest memories include plucking the strings of his guitar and listening to the low alto of my mother's voice as I sat on her lap, my head on her chest, as she harmonized. Divinity, Love, and art were already revealing their self-same source, even while I was being taught to think of them as different things.

Creativity leaked into and broke us free from our constraints. We struggled financially, barely scraping by. At times I caught my mom in tears, worried about the rising cost of rent. We moved countless times chasing affordable housing, dependent on the mission and raising our own support to survive. Most Christmases, there were no gifts. Other gifts shone: the Christmas Eve meal, the soft glow of candlelight, the scent of mandarin oranges, and the wonder present during that season. And so it is nothing short of miraculous that my parents managed to find a way for my brother and me to take art classes from an esteemed art master whose work hung in the Reina Sofia in Madrid and for me to take ballet classes. But, then, love always finds a way to make something out of nothing.

The countless hours of strenuous rehearsal and ballet training taught me creative resilience. My mother sitting patiently for hours and weathering the intensity of my tears and threats of quitting reminded me that the struggle was where art is made real. And then, on Saturdays, we had art lessons where my brother and I were blissfully rescued from the domain of rational, a weekly window of permission to trust and hone our devotion to our imagination.

We traveled as much as we could in our little blue Volvo. We'd buy a single baguette and some cheese and feast on the cliffs of Portugal or Normandy, watching the waves crash upon the rocks, our hair whipping in the wind. We'd collect shells and stones, "treasures," on the beaches as the fishermen mended their nets and the seagulls cried on with delight. We walked with hushed reverence through museums in Provence, Amsterdam, or Oslo and in famed artists' studios, where the smell of acrylics and oils and the bright-colored paint-splashed walls and floors said more to me than any theological treatise ever could about the nature of reality. My parents gave me the world by reverencing those who creatively gave themselves away.

These radical acts of generosity and intense love for the arts on the part of my parents will always be alive in me as their truest legacy and the heart of what made my childhood so rich despite the month-to-month struggle and uncertainty. They gave me the one thing I truly needed: love. The kind of love that imagines *more*. And they showed me what love does . . . *love creates.*

Spain was the ever-present backdrop, and so the core of my discovery of creativity was infused with the hues, flavors, and feeling of the country I call home. Earth of olive trees—brown, gold, and red; the aroma of Spanish tortilla and the slowness of long, savored meals; the palpable passionate tension between flamenco dancers and the closeness of greeting strangers with a kiss. Sights and scents of the erotic were as natural as life itself because cultures that appreciate life naturally love and bless every part of it.

I was twelve when we left Spain, but Spain lived on in every part of me. It was the dust in my lungs never exhaled, the flavors I metabolized into my very being, the lines my body made when I moved. Spain lived on in how I reached for my dad's guitar and wrote my first song, weaving a melody to hold the shattered pieces of my heart. Spain lived on in the set of my jaw and the proud tilt of my head and the curve of my hips. Spain lives on still in me . . . in the way I love so fiercely, in the way I make.

Over the years, I outgrew different religious containers like clothing . . . like too-tight shoes. Eventually, I threw off the constriction of the church altogether in favor of a more mystical, universal, and earthbound way of understanding reality. I trusted my bare feet instead, allowing my instincts to lead me beyond the enclosures of buildings, binaries, and exclusionary belonging out into a bigger, broader landscape. I began to trust my own heart, allowing life-force, Eros, to move me beyond familiarity into the Unknown beyond.

It is hard when you feel that for reasons you can't even fully name, what once worked about a belief system no longer does. When suddenly what used to feel like home feels suffocating, off, and wrong. It was a dark night of the soul, a crisis of faith. But the weird part was that even though it was so painful to leave behind the sense of belonging that religion had given me, with each step into the unknown wilderness of "I don't know," my experience of the sacred only became larger, clearer, more alive, and perceptible. Sitting on my bed surrounded by windows overlooking the hills of Silver Lake, Los Angeles, one morning, I penned the words to a song:

When I was a child
I pictured you, like my brother in the sun
Daring me to move.
A face like my mother's,
Hands like my father's, they covered mine.
And life was just fine.

When at last I grew, it was always with you
Me the dutiful good son, the obedient one.
It was the only way,
The only way I knew how to prove to you . . .
What I thought was true.

Soft is the hardest part,
Soft is the hardest part,
To give till you break, to open and let,
To make peace with pain . . . again and again,
Forgive me Lord, I didn't know . . . anything at all.

I had the worst time to make it . . . outside the warmest womb,
My heart was breaking, my altar left in ruins.
How long I waited, how long till you said,
"Up, you may get up . . . and walk."

To walk. What if our faith is actualized when we stop making it about beliefs and *courageously, simply live* into our own capacity and our own questions? Maybe faith becomes real the minute we walk and leave the institution. When we stop idolizing the steps someone else took. Maybe faith becomes real with each step we take, trusting our own journey as we walk deeper into the Unknown.

When I think of all the life that has ensued, my own creative expressions, all of my spiritual exploration and training, the hunger that has driven my curiosity, as well as all the creative unfurling of my personal life, musical career, painting, and now writing, what shaped me most is this basic orientation toward the courage of letting go of what we think we know to make room for what could be. The creative movement of love, of Eros, as it expands and moves toward the unimagined *more.* The radical, brave vulnerability required of the creative act defines the most meaningful moments of transformation in my life, whether they be moments of wonder or anguish . . . or sometimes both.

I have traveled many circuitous paths throughout my life, and none of the meanderings has been wasted time. But I have certainly experienced chapters of my life suppressing my creative instincts to live out the version of my life I thought I "should" live. I acquiesced to prescriptions from society and religion in my desire to please a script I had been handed. My life became hemmed in by these identities, these roles I played so well that I almost convinced myself it was what I wanted. It took a radical inner spiritual unknowing and unlearning revolution and outer practical re-centering of my creativity before I began to inhabit my own skin. Before I began to feel truly alive. Before I came home to myself, my desire, Eros . . . and through that homecoming I was finally able to allow love to do what love does: *create more.*

Whatever has been composted of my faith can be synthesized, simply, into this belief: *there is a coherent creative force that moves through everything.* What symbolizes that coherence to you might be God, The Universe, Source, Higher-Self, or simply Life. To me that animating, creative life-force is what I describe as Eros.

I hope these pages offer all of us a practical reframe of desire, to help us (re)member an embodied relational approach to a thriving, enlivened life. This creative desire is not for the sake of possession, certainty, or certitudes but rather a desire that, by its orientation to love, leads toward communion and creates more life. The call to this desire is also a call to set aside what so often hijacks true desire: certitudes driven by control and an instinct to dominate that which we fear—mainly, what we do not know. The Eros that I seek to animate in us all is a life-force that, in its commitment to life's flourishing, is unafraid of unknowing . . . is unafraid of *more.*

Eros moves us beyond the rational, beyond stories and narratives to describe and locate the messy magic of making in the midst of our (human and more-than-human) embodied creativity. That's why I focus here. The erotic provides an experiential field beyond the logics and systems we hide behind, beyond our excuses and fear of being fully alive.

My hope is that this perspective supports your journey toward your own life's flourishing, whatever your ground or belief. I'm intentionally presenting a poetic understanding of embodied creativity through a nonreligious framework for an ecological, relational approach to a meaningful life. Love (Eros/life-force) is in, part of, and for everyone. While the stories I share are born from my own body and experience as a cisgendered heterosexual female, this book is for anyone, for all genders, sexual orientations, for those who are religious or those who consider themselves agnostic or atheistic alike. This book is seeking to provide a worldview and field guide of erotic-creative practice for all.

Healthy religion orients us to wonder, awe and positions us in reverence to mystery. My experience, however, is that religion is more often limiting human imagination than animating it. Is it any wonder that I form part of the largest cohort that utilizes terms like *spiritual but not religious* to express the ambiguous postreligious landscape that so many of us would rather be lost in?

Still, it would be hubris to not recognize that religious traditions represent millennia of profound teaching, refined practices, and mystical truth . . . *spiritual technology*, as I like to call it, the best of which I would like to assert can be composted in service to our shared freedom and creativity. So while I do not speak from any religious identity myself, I occasionally draw from the spiritual technology in the mystical expressions of religion. And I place spiritual insights in tension and relationship with the human works of great artists, painters, musicians, and poets throughout the ages, whom I also consider mystic revolutionaries of creative possibility.

My experience has taught me again and again (and continues to do so) that when knowledge and certitudes, and the identities that emerge from those static entrenched ideas, are no longer the aim, we are freed to let go of what we thought we knew and welcome a whole new possibility for what could be. The body then becomes the central vehicle of our experiencing an earthy, present, fleshy connection to a larger sense of inherent worth and creative freedom.

"Completion" or "arrival" is not the goal. The idea of completion is an illusory arrival point. In a creative life, the goal shifts from such arbitrary future destinations or outcomes into the intimacy of the immediate present act of *making*. When we awaken to this purpose, our daily focus is simply to be as creative as we can, in every moment, understanding that such a stance is what is required for all great contributions and deepening relations . . . in love, justice, and art.

Eros moves through desire as it seeks to make new connections, transform, and make. That life-force beckons us to courageously live and love from the absolute freedom that enables ever greater love and more life. A shared ethics of mutual enlivenment is the outcome of that freedom, in which "you" and "I" become "we."

This experimental field has its mentors, some I'm fortunate enough to call my friends. The philosophy and friendship and work on erotic ecology of Dr. Andreas Weber and the mischievous marvel of Dr. Bayo Akomolafe's unknowing-ways have been hugely influential in my thinking, both in their writing and in conversation, evidenced in my references throughout this book. And while I sadly never got to meet the great philosopher and mystic Beatrice Bruteau, her work and impact are likewise felt through the explorations on these pages.

Each of these thinkers helped me realize how Eros has been culturally relegated to the bedroom, so instead of understanding all of life as erotic—as full of divine throbbing, pulsing, relationality, pleasure, and possibility—we have limited that erotic power to one aspect of humanity and once again anthropomorphized another facet of our shared ecological reality and creative potential. We sent Eros to the bedroom and tied its potential up to the bed. Not that the Erotic doesn't rule the sexual domain, but it is also *so much more* than that.

What if we could respond to this fundamental life-energy of desire by remembering its natural aim, which is *to make more life?* If life's natural aim is to make more abundant life, then it follows that our lives will also be a progression of outgrowing spiritual containers, expanding beyond communities of belonging and pushing past the edges of our own familiar maps. Eros does not heed the lines and too-small shapes that dominant culture has prescribed for us.

Eros's aim is to courageously give itself away, to pour itself out like libations for the sake of anointing the possibility that new life heralds. That's why I believe it is *creativity* that marks the site of integration and true transformation. Transformation may begin with a shift in perspectives, in changing one's mind, but it is metabolized, lived out, and marked by how that shift in perspectives impacts your desire, capacity, and freedom to create, animate, and generate more life. You are *what you make.*

Like the line in that song I wrote in my room in Silver Lake, it seems that Eros (life-force, Source, or whatever other term constitutes the Relational Whole of the Universe for you) is constantly calling us to recognize our own potential, our own agency, our own creative courage . . . whispering to us, "*Walk! You can get up . . . and walk.*" Break out of the too-small shapes you've confined yourself in, it seems to say; believe you are as capable of making new worlds as I am.

This book is therefore pointless if it doesn't lead to the embodiment of these erotic principles amid your lived experience, a metabolization into everyday choices that opens you up to a creatively enlivened life. So what can this practically mean for you when you're dealing with your obnoxious boss, seeking to deepen your relationship with your partner, or attempting to work up the courage to put yourself out there in a creative offering?

It means you may begin to reframe how you think about what constitutes a meaningful life. It means you might reconsider the intensity of the tension you experience daily; any and all tensions (difference, longing, challenge, otherness, not-knowing, uncertainty) may no longer be a problem that needs to be fixed but instead reverenced as playing a part in the process of creativity. Suddenly, you may discover that what you thought was a problem is just part of the creative cycle as it opens up new possibilities in your life.

I'll say more on how that does not excuse, condone, or romanticize evil or injustice but rather creatively subverts and revolutionizes how we think about the impasses, disagreements, blocks, and seemingly insurmountable challenges in our lives, small and large, personal and collective. Whether in our romantic partnerships, friendships, work life, creative projects, or in our collective frustration with systemic injustice and the corrupt consumeristic destruction of our shared life on this planet, the creative invitation is to recognize the ache of our longing, frustration, anguish not as some temporal obstacle that needs to be overcome. Rather, the ache is understood as what makes, as what creatively gives rise to a greater imagination and shared life. As the revolution of transmuting our suffering into great art. And in so doing, liberates ourselves and each other from what-has-been into what-could-be.

It means that instead of being terrified by uncertainty and unknowing, we embrace these as the preexistent condition for moreness, creativity, and life. Desire and longing cease to be for the sake of "arrival" or possession or projection of a subject-object split and instead are understood as the bass line that runs under all of life, as the fundamental function of the open-ended question of life's unpredictable unknowability.

In Dr. Emily Nagoski's bestselling book on sexuality, *Come as You Are*, she lays out the core categories of what leads to great sex: context, good communication, and embodied presence to pleasurable sensation.

While my hope is that this entire book constitutes the category of helpful communication on how to shift into more erotic-creative life, you could think of the first half of this book as setting up *the context* for that shift and the second half of the book as *the practice* of embodying it, being present to it, and discovering pleasurable possibility in the midst of your daily life.

The first part of the book explores what I mean by *Eros* and how it can be understood as a worldview or philosophy—as a whole set of wisdom practices and an orientation of life. So the first five chapters will share this erotic-creative wisdom in a way that can hopefully enliven not just your life but also the reciprocal web of relationships you form part of. In the second half of the book, I outline daily practices of the creative life, exploring simple tenets for the erotic-creative life in little mantra-like principles you can test out and play with in practice in your own relationships and creative projects alike. Because of that, you can choose your own adventure. If you want to dive into the practical material first and save the bigger paradigm stuff for later, go for it!

I hope that this book is first and foremost useful in your love life, your friendships, parenting, and especially in your creative yearning to give more of yourself away as an act of pleasurable possibility. The reason I hold this hope is that I am offering you what has proven most useful to a greater enlivening in my own relationships and creative expressions. I write to you not as an expert but as a fellow unknowing poet-troubadour on the path with you. I am sharing the hints and guesses that are helping me most as I continue to learn how to give more and more of myself away in creativity and love. These are the principles that have helped me transform how I think about the menial, mundane, and even sometimes frustrating aspects of life into a life that is fully turned on, erotically enlivened through presence, pleasure, and playfulness.

This book was written as summer slowly shed its vibrancy and delicately surrendered to the unknowing letting go of autumn and as autumn became silent under the blankets of snow in early winter. It was written from my home in Michigan, beneath the maple and oak trees that stand gentle guard beside my house and ground me daily. It was written through the welcome and constant interruption of my kids, thankfully grounded from any esoteric abstraction by their experiences, needs, and wonderful imaginations. It was written on the road, in New York City and Los Angeles, as I continued to perform shows with my band and worked on my next record. It was written between brush strokes of paintings, colorful works that gratefully invited me into the blissful relief of the nonverbal. But it was also written before this time, through my childhood in Spain. It was written through countless conversations with friends, colleagues, and lovers. It was written through every love, loss, beginning, and ending. It was written in every moment of my life thus far and in each of the Polaroid vignettes in the Overture.

This book is writing itself through me still, into greater unknowing creative possibilities. It is an offering that will become more than me as part of you, which is just how any creative offering should be in transcending the limited container of words, pages, canvas, or recordings into shared enlivenment.

Each of us is always, ever writing the masterpiece of our lives with every choice we make, with each touch, look, laugh, and tear. With every turn toward hope instead of despair, with each turn toward unimagined possibility instead of the comfort of predictability. I hope this book serves your creative courage to make the most of this precious life . . . to not hold anything back, to not let fear hem you in with certitudes or limiting identities or narratives.

Regardless of your vocation, you, darling, are an artist . . . and your masterpiece is you, as you courageously continue to become. But so many of us choose to stay hidden, half-living in the pressure-filled conformity of a "should" life, hemmed in on every side of a life resembling a hamster wheel, perpetually seeking achievement or affirmation, plugged into our phones 24/7, disconnected from the environment, disassociated from our bodies, and disengaged from our truest potential. Before we can get to that pleasure-filled presence and unfurled potential, there is a lot that needs to be unlearned and reframed.

I often get asked how it is that I practically live such a creative life of uncertainty amid the demands of being a single mom. How I harmonize the life of working as a recording artist with the mystical. How is it that I can be both a wildly sensual and feminine performer and be devoted to a life of philosophical reflection and contemplation? I tend to smile when I get these questions, the corners of my mouth rising coyly in a Mona Lisa way, like I've got a secret. And the truth is . . . I do. The answer to that question of how it is that I metabolize a path of love, creativity, and possibility in the midst of everyday life is really simple . . .

Everything is Erotic.

Or, at least . . . *it can be.* My hope with this book is to demonstrate how.

Act I

An Erotic Worldview Shift

From Control to Creativity

Chapter One

Eros
The Art of Relating

Art must be an expression of love or it is nothing.

—Marc Chagall

I sat under the shade of a bush that had grown through the rocks and stared at the blindingly silver Mediterranean Sea and white sandy beach ahead. The sun was already high in the sky, and the sound of fishermen down the beach trailed up to me in an undifferentiated joyful cacophony. Alexandria was humming to full life. It wasn't hard for me—at nineteen—to feel the history of this place. It radiated off the ground and spoke from the coastal architecture. I stretched my legs out into the sun as I pulled a different sort of perfect radiant orb from my bag . . . an orange. Not just any orange. But a fresh giant globe of an orange a woman had brought from her own grove in baskets to share. She cupped my face when she handed it to me, smiling and saying something in Arabic I didn't understand.

I held the orange sun in my hand and began to peel off the rind. Sharp citrus oils burst in a baptismal spray into the air and mixed with the smell of salt and sea on the cool breeze. When this work was done, I looked at one single slice of orange. Really *looked* at it. The little sinews that looked like my own muscles, the way the light made it glow amber . . . the delicate translucent thin skin that covered and held its bursting secrets. As I bit into it, the sun yielded itself in a supernova that exploded into my mouth. I was eating the sun itself. It was so good that it startled me. I wanted more. Another gust of cool breeze blew my hair into my face, and my sticky hand anointed my own forehead as I pushed the stray veil strands away, finishing the slice and savoring it . . . laughing in delight.

I continued like this, in absolute erotic rapture, slice after slice. Something of nature was revealing itself to me, an ever-present and immediate physical intimacy I had not yet known. What this embodied experiential awareness revealed couldn't be hidden: this life, this earth, is humming with relationship, history, memory, meaning. An energy singing itself in every atom, particle of sand, sinew of an orange. Salt, citrus, eucalyptus . . . scents of utter seduction.

And the more present I became to partaking in this holy communion, the more nature imparted herself to me. I wasn't just eating an orange. I was becoming one with it and through it, every relationship it represented . . . from the woman who brought them, to her grove, to the soil they grew on, to the rain and sun that grew them. Through the orange, I was ecstatically touching Alexandria herself, and she was touching me . . . changing me, transforming me. The breeze became her hand and the sun her heat. Juice dripping down my chin, I laughed at the pleasure-filled wonder of this life.

And no, I'm not in ecstasy every time I eat a piece of fruit since that experience of biological orgasmic oneness. But the moment never left me because it was the beginning of discovering Eros as ever present in every facet of my life on this planet. In that moment I finally experientially understood Eros as the humming relationality of the universe—the energetic seeking, longing, and finding of connection in the creation of complexity. Eros is the hunger for more, the frustration of what is, and the yearning for what could be as it seeks to create, make, build, express. In that moment I finally felt how Eros *is* creativity, although the intuition had been brewing in me my entire life.

At three years old, I declared to my mother that I was going to be a star. "What does that mean, honey?" she asked. "You know . . . when you stand in front of everyone, and they all clap and love you." She thought this was so funny that she wrote it down in a baby book.

It makes me cringe a little to share this with you, but it's also cute and adorable in that unapologetic way that kids speak. Now that I'm a mom, I've written down similar proclamations from my own kids with a sense of wonder at the unique script written in their souls. These occasional declarations uttered by little kids strike me as holy somehow. Past what could be seen as a charmingly childish statement, something core to their hearts is being shared.

Thinking back on my own admission, I'm mystified and fascinated by my choice of words. Why did I say "star" and not "singer" or "ballerina" or "painter"? Why did I say "stand in front of everyone" and not say "when you're in the movies" or "singing on a stage"? And why were the outcomes "clapping" and "love"? What did that mean to my three-year-old self?

I have a freakish memory that extends all the way back to my toddler years and recall the hushed reverence and feeling of mystery, awe, and wonder that possessed me when I considered who I wanted to be in the world, even back at age three. We didn't have a television; I hadn't even gone to a live ballet performance, theater, movie, or concert at that age. So where did this idea come from? I cannot say how, but I remember being already absolutely certain that artists were akin to the fantastical characters in the children's books my parents read me. Somehow I knew that *artists had magic.*

My definition of art magic included three clues about creating that I can now confirm: it had something to do with the light of stars, being willing to bare your soul before others, and the way vulnerability can inspire joy and wonder. This art magic, I knew, was inextricably related to love somehow.

Art is our human longing translated into an external gift that expresses something vulnerable, true, resonant, and inspiring. Art is all about *relating*. Relating can be understood in two different ways: as narrating or telling someone something or as the quality of resonating or identifying with something being shared. And Art is a relating that includes both definitions: it both narrates something personal in the artist's experience and soul and also, through the art form, creates and establishes a channel allowing the personal to become universally resonant. In other words, art creates connection. It reaches out beyond the artist into the ether like threads of a web floating in the wind, seeking purchase, like root systems seeking other roots beneath the ground, longing to grow, reach, receive, touch, know, and be known. In this way, art is fueled by the desire of *love*.

Sitting down to write a song or paragraph, or standing before a blank canvas, I can promise you that seeking approval, arrival, or achievement is the furthest thing from my mind and body.

When I write a song, my eyes close as I hold my arms around the great wooden instrument that is bigger than my frame. My well-calloused fingers move around the fret board, moving from one shape to the next, searching . . . as my right hand strums and stops . . . strums and stops. I hum a little bit . . . and a little bit more.

Returning to that chord progression again and again, as if willing the initial melody manifestation to concretize, my voice gains confidence . . . then grows soft once more as I begin again to search for the next note, and the next . . . almost as if groping in the dark for the shape I might recognize. On and on the process goes. Listening, trying . . . stopping, writing down . . . repeating. Hugging the great curved box vibrating against my chest as the vessel on the voyage of my own making. I, the explorer, forever scanning the horizon of resonance deep within, waiting to hear and feel the melody that is still waiting to be sung.

The interesting thing is that when the melody starts to really take shape, there is a vague recognition, a strange familiarity. The awareness is both known and unknown. Like finding a new way home.

When I make, I take the posture of prayer, of a supplicant, of a devoted lover. I take my time, I move slow, and I feel every touch of my fingers on the strings, or the brush on the canvas, or the sweet ache of my muscles. I approach with reverence, with awe and wonder. I never know what is going to happen. I offer myself, body and soul, to the making, and the making makes me come alive.

What possesses my body and being is a loving longing, an objectless yearning that burns bright and hot within me. A desire that isn't about an outcome. I'm too focused on tuning into the frequency of that source of magic, that "other place" from which beauty is born. My whole body and mind are devoted to becoming a vessel that can serve as a conduit, so "I" have to get out of the way. Single-minded in my listening and in my drawing, writing, painting, singing . . . like a hunter, I seek a shape in the dark that has yet to emerge but I know it is there. I pursue it like a starved lover catching a glimpse of their beloved. An arrow is shot straight from my heart over the bow of this world into the next, from what has been to what could be. And like Cupid, I wait for it to hit its mark and for the spell to take effect.

What drives me in those quiet, intimate moments is devotion to serving the expression and to giving myself away in every way possible. To throw my whole soul and body into the fury of the offering. Hours will pass, and I won't notice, too consumed in the movement to stop. Sometimes I wrestle the making down, and sometimes it pins *me* down. With every breath, with every inhale and exhale, I chase it . . . and seduce it. I listen and I express. I give and I receive.

When I am making, I am making love.

This is no metaphor, but the metaphor happens to work. The process of making correlates with the sexual act. Both are born from love and are in service to creativity. The tension of attraction. The bearing of yearning. The all-consuming, singular focus and passion. The simmering arousal and seduction. The intimacy and immediacy of vulnerability. The tangle of expression and surrender. The quickened breath at the verge of inspired flight. The pressure and release of a devoted adoration that moves you into ecstasy (from the Greek *ekstasis*, meaning "standing outside yourself"), into touching on that which is both you *and* more-than-you.

Over the years, my art-making has taken many forms. And in this book, I share many of my experiences—from early iterations in my life in ballet and painting, music and writing, to the ultimate realm of artistic creativity: relationships.

Yes, you read that right.

Relationships are artistic expressions. Why? Because love requires the same stance that art does: the radical choice to cocreate something new every day through courageous vulnerability with the faith and hope of a shared imagination. The same devotion and willingness to see the other as mystery through the eyes of a beginner's mind. The same brave undressing and baring of our souls and bodies in our willingness to see and be seen. Touch and be touched. To inspire and be inspired.

This creative art magic isn't relegated to those who identify as artists but belongs to us all. Creativity *is* Eros, which is life itself. Eros is the creative energy of longing expressed in the generosity and generativity of love. Eros is the yearning to move and be moved, to express and receive, to connect and relate and resonate. Eros is the hunger for creative reciprocity to change and be changed, to be spent and be filled, to be undone and remade. Eros is the desire that drives us to create new possibilities, not to default or control or possess. Eros is the burning in your own heart that is perpetually calling you out of what is known and into the horizons of the unknown.

That means that the Erotic (love, creativity, life) also requires a dying to or letting go of what has been to make room for what could be. The Erotic (love, creativity, life) requires befriending the unknown, for the unknown is the unimagined "may be" and "could become." All lovers and makers must turn to this kind of courage in the act of loving and making. Eros requires vulnerability, for only through vulnerability can any experience resonate and nourish more love, creativity, life. Vulnerability serves as a radio frequency, a sonic bridge, that allows the experience to travel out beyond one's known self, into a shared beyond. Only when we are willing to *really* feel, allowing our hearts to vibrate with what is within—with every aching, fleshy, tenderness—can that inner resonance but burst into outer manifest expression. Like a song. Like love. Like magic.

And like a song, the sound waves reverberate forever. For Eros, completion, or even wholeness, is not the goal. *Creativity is.* Everything is always in process, unfinished, an aperture of possibility cracked open like a door to more. Longing, then, is not the dissatisfied feeling of yearning for satiety or completion but rather love's fundamental fuel to *create.*

This perspective doesn't apply simply to human creativity and imagination but—surprisingly—is a deeply ecological approach to life on this planet. Biologist and eco-philosopher Andreas Weber describes Eros as the thrumming relationality of the earth itself, the biological principle of reality that functions in and through every attraction, relation, and creation: "Eros is the principle of creative plenitude, the principle of superfluity, of sharing, of communication, of the self-actualization that lies dormant even in rocks and minerals. . . . Love is not a pleasant feeling, but the practical principle of creative enlivenment."

In *Matter and Desire: An Erotic Ecology*, Weber writes about the most radical ecological act we can embark on: falling in love with this earth and deepening our relationship with everything around us. This isn't an abstraction of love. His invitation is literally to deepen our relationships with the trees, birds, flowers, and everything more-than-human with which we cohabitate—and to see them all as kin. To move toward reverencing what is all around us in rapt attention as the soulful appreciation, respect, wonder, and care that love engenders. To awaken our senses to the extraordinary ordinary life all around us and allow ourselves to both literally and figuratively be touched by it. Weber's message could not be more timely or vital.

Our ecological crisis, social inequity, political vitriol and division all urgently demand we approach life differently. We have already destroyed our planet in irreversible ways and are seemingly hell-bent on deepening our entrenched binaries of hate that only lead to more suffering and loss of life.

It's easy to feel like these collective monsters are too big for us to slay or feel powerless in the face of the institutions that animate them. It doesn't help that we are constantly bombarded with news and feeds on our phones and with algorithm silos that perpetuate our divisions by discrediting whatever the other side believes. And then, because capitalism knows how to turn our despair into dollars, we are quickly fed images that distract us while incurring feelings of inferiority and of not being enough.

Overwhelm. Depress. Discredit. Distract. Deplete. Dangle false solutions to get your dollars.

Rinse and repeat.

The pattern is so engrained and so unconscious we don't even realize it's happening. It's as if the stars in our sky have been snuffed out one by one or perhaps faded so gradually we don't even notice . . . until we cannot find our way and feel lost in a blindness of our own making.

This is an artificial obscuring, the way city lights make it hard for our eyes to see the song of the stars above us. The convenience of electricity, too-bright screens, and distraction feeds dominate our sight until we believe it's normal to always be available, always online. *Don't ever unplug! Keep producing and fulfilling the insatiable expectation of a nonstop life*! Our vision is so exhausted, is it any wonder we can no longer see the world clearly, let alone the horizon of our own potential?

Sure, there are moments of wild magic that remind us of the big sky, but mostly it's the feeling stuck in the routines and the roles we don't remember choosing that remains. Perhaps on occasion, there is the recollection of having had dreams of a big life, a joyful, pleasurable, free, and wild life, but now that seems so far away, like a vision we read about in a book or dreamt of.

How did I get *here*? We wonder silently. How did I lose that freer, more creative and vibrant version of *me*? How did I lose aliveness, connection, *magic?* It's rarely a sudden thing. The dimming is often gradual. But sometimes it takes the lights going all the way out to remember the light within.

I was thirty-five when—in the midst of profound tragedy—my nearly ten-year marriage ended with the father of my two kids. The choice very much felt like a life-or-death situation. And I knew it. There was a tragic, traumatic reason for this, but that more obvious tragedy was stacked upon *decades* of the quiet internalized spiritual and gender normative expectations, prescribed roles that wore me down, like a microdose of poison daily ingested. My soul had gotten so anemic and so used to sipping smaller and smaller breaths, I nearly suffocated. There were millions of ways that I slowly lost myself . . . that I acquiesced to the expectation of compressing, minimizing, redirecting, and shelving my creativity, of extinguishing my life-force. Add to that a lethal dose of traumatic silencing that I experienced, and the flame that was once "me" was merely an ember glow on the verge of being snuffed out.

When I finally told my parents my decision to divorce, I closed my eyes as I spoke. I couldn't bear to see their disappointment. But when I looked up, my dad had tears streaming down his face. To my great surprise, these weren't tears of disappointment but *relief*. "Brie," he said, "I feel like you've been under this heavy, dark cloak . . . and listening to you now, I finally caught a glimpse of you again . . . like you are beginning your journey of healing, and the dark cloak might one day come off."

I hadn't touched my guitar in years. I hadn't painted in over a decade. I lived in black and white . . . literally. I had decorated in a modern, minimal, austere grayscale. I had lost twelve pounds, and on my frame, that was enough to make me look like a walking ghost. The ember sputtered on my vibrancy, on my art, on *me*.

Shedding that heavy, dark cloak and finding my way back to me took many years. I held on to a vision like an icon of the woman I knew I could be, the wild, free, creative, and joyfully vibrant girl I had almost lost.

Wandering through a dark forest in the middle of the night, with nothing to guide me but the light of the stars above, I felt lost. And I felt exposed, scraped raw, trusting in the strength of my own vulnerability as I took one step into the unknown forest and then the next, determined to find myself again, determined to go my own way. Little by little, I began to recognize myself again. And little by little, I began to heal and eventually found my way to a life of love, relatedness, inspiration, and creativity beyond what I could have imagined for myself.

Those years were nothing short of being remade in the ashes . . . of the oxygen of love and life and hope turning to flame again through absolute tenacity. It was the daily courageous choice that my ex and I held on to in our commitment to divorce in the most conscious, compassionate, and generous way possible. To allow our love to shift into a new shape. It was my devotion to my kids in believing that what they most needed from me was a mother who was passionately and fully alive. It was my willingness to compost old belief systems in favor of a living, authentic, related way of being and becoming in this world.

It was letting go of everything I thought I knew to make room for what could be. It was the alchemy of creativity—of love and life as it shifted into more love and more life.

Refusing to give up on the dream of your most enlivened life is what this book is about. I hope some part of you knows that it's still possible. The same part of you that wants off of that hamster wheel of scarcity and assigned societal expectations and is hungry for that creative, abundant life. That part of you knows that if you could learn how to live a pleasure-filled life fully "turned on," it wouldn't just be fulfilling and flourishing but also a radical act of an alternative social revolution.

When we discover a deeper relatedness with ourselves, we deepen our connection with others and the planet. As we become enlivened in ways that also enliven others, we grow more wildly generative in our creative work. The discovery of erotic-creative principles helped me through that night forest passage and continues to fill my life with presence, pleasure, and possibility. Sharing them with you is my way of passing you my telescope, of helping you remember that bigger sky beyond what your eyes can now see.

Maybe like me, you want a life so caught up in the erotic thrall of making more love that it bursts out of your heart like light from the nuclear fusion of a star. I'm absolutely convinced that the path to the greatest soul-stirring possibility requires radical and brave vulnerability. And beyond a shadow of a doubt, that kind of courage inspires and animates a creative hope and possibility in all of us and in this world. And yeah, that's something I'm cheering for . . . and I'd bet you are, too, because you picked up this book for a reason.

So perhaps my three-year-old self was right, after all. But here's the thing: we're *all* meant to burn as brightly and fervently as the constellations above us. Before you gag on Disney dust, though, know this: the only reason stars shine is because nuclear fusion is essentially a process of stars crushing inward on themselves as they give themselves away. So this erotic-creative mindset shift requires the gravity of our willingness to look within and collapse those internalized narratives that are hemming us in and holding us back in the presumed safety of a small, scripted life.

This shift also requires us to look at where and how we withhold, where we're too busy protecting our fragile egos instead of generously giving ourselves away. I won't dress this up for you: looking at those internalized narratives may feel like a crushing, a dying, and an undoing. And it is. But it's also kind of (and literally) *hot.* All that pressure is an erotic kind of mounting tension, an ecstatic letting go and being undone in a way that will create an incredible amount of energy until you're so lit up and alive and turned on that you could be spotted galaxies away.

If there are things in this book that shock you or shake you . . . good. If you find my framing around eroticism a little uncomfortable, cool. I'm okay with that. As we'll explore, the "unholy" trinity of the erotic, the feminine or nonbinary, and the divergently creative has been suppressed and conflated as something "shameful" in spiritual and religious circles as though they ought to be covered up, hidden, and not spoken about, which is usually how the patriarchy responds to anything that threatens its dominant status. And it's precisely because these three ingredients are related in the recipe of life-making-more-life that each must be reclaimed and restored to its rightful place as part of our divine (if you believe in such) right to critique what isn't working in society by creating something better.

So you may feel twitchy about the categorical comparisons I am making between the erotic and creativity, between sex and spiritual/personal growth, between lovemaking and making the world a better place. To me, the erotic *is* creativity, which *is* life. Which means the terms and metaphors are all earthy, luscious, sensual, applicable, and (mostly) interchangeable. It may take you a minute to feel comfortable doing the same, and that's okay. Notice what it is that riles you up as much as what resonates. Both what attracts us and what repels us are great teachers.

If I had to guess at a core desire you and I likely have in common, it would be that neither of us is interested in a half-lived life. We're all done playing it safe; being a good, sweet whatever; and living a docile, spiritually neutered life. Most of us have grown up witnessing the harm caused by the dualities that separate mind from body, body from spirit, body from environment, and self from other. I'm willing to bet that we are both wanting a spirituality that is as fleshy, earthbound, sensual, feeling, fierce, and creative as we are. There is an undeniable collective hunger for whatever we practice to not only animate our individual potential but also help us become more deeply related to everyone on this earth, to make us kinder, more compassionate, more enlivened, and capable of inspiring others to feel the same.

This hunger is driven by a dawning realization that a life of achievement, or arrival-oriented ambitions that leave us exhausted, depleted, depressed, or burned out is not the "good" life . Those "one day" maps do not reveal the hidden treasure of the bountiful and pleasurable plenty, here and now. I have long since stopped using the maps for approval or validation outside of myself, both in my art and in my personal life. These aren't my motivators for my life-force, for creativity. What does motivate me is the preciousness of this gift, of this life . . . in this moment. If I'm lucky enough to live into old age, I know that I don't want to wake up one day wishing I had actually had the courage to color outside the prescribed professional, institutional, or social lines. That I had the courage to live a thriving life of pleasure, presence, and playfulness. I don't want to reach the end of my life with the bitterness of regret, knowing I could have given more of myself away in love. In the words of poet Mary Oliver, "I don't want to end up simply having visited this world."

I want the supernova. The big magic now. The wow. The permission-granting, contagious freedom. The wild wonderful. The seductively sensual. The revolution of reciprocal enlivenment. I want to leave this life knowing I really, *truly* loved and lived an inspired life that inspired more life. I want to leave this life knowing I fully gave my life away.

If you feel this way, too, then I hope these pages help you chart a new constellation, one that can help you find your way home to yourself.

I must warn you, however, that Eros doesn't move in predictable equations or linear progressions. This isn't one of those "seven simple steps to your most erotic life" kind of books. Oftentimes, what's in the way *is* the way, and the cavernous cracks of our own heartbreak often serve as the vaginal rifts for our own emergence and birth. Chaos is, after all, the mother of Eros. So, if you really are wanting to live your most enlivened life, be ready for things to get messy.

Chapter Two

Creative Chaos
Being Undone and Remade by Love

Every act of creation is first of all an act of destruction.
—Pablo Picasso

At my desk, I worked on coloring in the map. I angled my colored pencil so that the pigment would be light, keeping my strokes even. Then outlined the whole thing with the same color but now pressing in so the intense color on the edges would neatly contain the diffused color inside.

Lines. The human world is defined by lines. By borders. By clear demarcations. By shapes with corresponding definitions. This is a circle. This is a square. This is the United States of America. This is Spain. This is the distance on a map of lines between the country you were born in and the one you call home.

My teacher, Don Ezequiel, picked up my map and declared to the whole class, "Now this, class, is a *map*. Take note of how Gabi perfectly traced each country and how cleanly she colored them and labeled them. This is exactly what I am looking for." He placed the map back on my desk and kept walking down the row. Embarrassed by the attention but pleased by the praise, I felt my face redden as I kept coloring neatly . . . always inside the lines.

Lines. My life was defined by lines. Lines I couldn't cross. Lines that separated me from others. Lines that separated me from God. Lines between good and bad. Lines that declared where I belonged and where I didn't. Lines that created the shape of the life I was told I should want. And since I was told to color inside the lines, I did.

From an early age, we are taught to do precisely this. It's almost difficult now to remember where we first learned it. Learned to angle the colored pencil and fill in the shapes lightly . . . not too much pigment. Softly because you're not supposed to want the hue of your life to be too dark, too loud, too strong. You know . . . keep it pretty, reasonable, palatable, pleasing. Don't be aggressive. Don't be too passionate. Don't be messy. Just . . . stay within the lines you're given, okay? That's it. Good girl.

The problem is . . . something inside us *knows better.* Something inside us *remembers.* A stirring inside us recalls the joyful permission of finger paint, of making a mess, and of shapes not needing to correspond to rational ideas. Something strains against the borders that contain and constrain us and whisper to us of the wild freedom we once felt when we allowed ourselves to play and *imagine more* than what "was" . . . watching like a wild animal, waiting for the moment the cage door of our lines opens, for the moment when we let our colors bleed beyond the edges. When we finally dare to shatter the lines or when our hearts break, and the lines shift and become fragmented like a kaleidoscope. Like a cubist dream.

I was six or seven years old when I first met Picasso. The Reina Sofia Museum in Madrid was one of my parents' favorites, and since we were dutifully dragged to every art museum to take in the Impressionists since the time I could waddle, we were finally deemed ready for Picasso's cubism.

I was transfixed. Color, wild riots of dense pigment and noncorresponding shapes, alien shapes, lines that didn't move according to the script of *how things were supposed to look.* This was not the soft, blurred impressionist colors and edges of Monet and Degas. No, this was . . . this was *passion.* This was *intensity. Freedom. Wild. Permission. More.*

This was alive.

Of course, I didn't have those words yet. I just knew my eyes couldn't get enough. It felt like my whole soul was drinking, guzzling down every painting . . . absorbing something vital that I had been starving for—dying for. Something that was shattering something in me and saving my life.

I recall the way chills ran up my spine as we stepped into the room with a single giant, mural-sized Picasso in black and white, the famed *Guernica.* Even in black and white, Picasso screamed his fury, his heartbreak. My tiny body dwarfed before the massive painting, I stood and stared and stared and stared at the chaos, at the sharp edges of pain and sorrow, the total destruction caused by the bombing by Franco and Hitler on this innocent village of civilians in the middle of the night.

My parents and brother moved on, but I stayed glued to the spot. I kept looking at the knife-like pointed triangle shape coming out of the horse's mouth. All I could think was, *How did he know exactly what a scream looks like . . . what it feels like . . . when it's frozen and stuck inside?*

* * *

Eros isn't all oranges in Alexandria or the thrall of passionate songwriting, painting, or creating. The voracious, consuming hunger of life sometimes destroys and unmakes what has been so something new can be born. It pushes us into the depths of our discomfort with uncertainty and forces us to reckon with chaos and the depths of what we do not know.

Eros does not play by the rules of order . . . it makes messes out of our clear categories and lines and at times is hell-bent on undoing and unmaking to make something new. I offer myself amid one of my "creative hurricanes" (as my friends call them) as exhibit A. Usually, I have forgotten to eat and shower, and I look like I'm sporting Albert Einstein hair like it's the latest trend. If I'm painting, the kitchen turns into my studio, with paint and plaster everywhere. If I'm recording, my cable management in my studio looks like I'm wading in a tangle two feet deep of snakes. Chaos and Eros are related. They go together, apparently since the beginning.

The arrival of Chaos and Eros in our human consciousness came through Greek mythology. The ancient Greeks depict Chaos as the female unfathomable void of emptiness at the beginning of time, described by Hesiod as a bottomless chasm from which sprung Gaia (earth), Tartarus (the Underworld), and Eros (Love).

Eros, however, was not the cute cherub cupid of the later Romans that the ancient Greeks described but rather a primordial force present at the very creation of the earth itself—a terrifying, dark, and potentially destructive energy. Hesiod describes Eros as "a force of nature, one of the fundamental primal building blocks of the cosmos."

Throughout Greek literature, Eros is depicted as terrible and terrifying, described by Plato as "the puppet's strings" that make us move or declared the "most unconquerable" God and "tyrant of gods of men" by Euripides. Metaphors describe Eros as a storm, wind, fire, sea, and disease or madness—all things that represented upheaval and certain death or destruction to ancient civilization.

Eros was described as the life-force animating sexual desire and, as such, attacked the rational mind, disrupted order, and even created social upheaval. To the ancients, this longing-born-of-chaos was not the romantic concept we have today but the archetype of the monstrous that at all times needed to be fought against; held at bay; conquered through reason, order, and control. Eros, the unknown monster-maker, was cast since antiquity as humanity's most ancient foe . . . as the force of nature herself.

And what do we do when we are afraid of what we do not know? That which terrifies us because it is made more powerful by its unknowability? We try to dominate it. Subjugate it. Control it.

But Eros, like nature, like our hearts, cannot be tamed.

We could say that Eros is essentially the great disruptor of our ideas of order. The ultimate trickster that interrupts our plans. But Eros is not chaos for the sake of chaos but rather the chaos that is part of creating something new. The wild, untamable monster-maker Eros has been a shape-shifter across epochs and civilizations. Just about every culture and tradition has a monster-maker myth with a concordant story of human efforts to dominate, tame, or slay it.

We see hints of the same terrifying, unknown monster-maker in Tiamat, ancient Mesopotamian mythology, the fearsome primordial goddess who reigned over the chaos of creation at the heart of the salt sea and was mother of the gods. She is formlessly vague in the *Enuma Elish*, depicted sometimes as a woman and sometimes as a body of water and occasionally as a creature with a tail. Later, this shape-shifting quality of hers caused her to be depicted as that which slithers between the worlds of land and water—a serpent. Or between sea and sky as a sea dragon. (Apparently, anything that is queerly at home in simultaneous worlds or expressions has been monstrous to humanity from the beginning.)

Theologian and scholar Catherine Keller describes a harmonic relationship between the primordial, chaotic, messy, fluid, "deep" origins of the creation of the Mesopotamian Tiamat with the Tehom (the deep, dark, oceanic abyss) of the Hebrew origin story. She notes historical occurrences of "the deep" chaos-maker origin stories in her book *Face of the Deep: A Theology of Becoming*. One such story is the Pelagian myth of the goddess Eurynome—from whom the world-egg was birthed—who created the north wind by dancing on the dark waters of the ocean, the wind twining around her like a snake.

Then there is Lilith, whose monstrous footprints begin in Sumerian and Mesopotamian origins as a goddess of fertility, but in the Judaic mystical Zohar, she is depicted as Adam's first wife.

This woman who was formed from the filth and muck of the earth was apparently too problematic and opinionated for Adam. Eventually, she decides she's had enough, sprouts wings, and leaves the garden of male-ordered perfection. When God sends angels to retrieve her, she refuses her place at the paradise of patriarchy and chooses instead to become the mother of demons, happy instead to become—in the words of Dr. Bayo Akomolafe—"the primal womb of the inappropriate."

There is the Hindu goddess Kali, the wild destroyer and liberator who is depicted as wearing a skirt of severed limbs and a necklace of decapitated heads, worshipped in Tantric sects as the Divine mother, mother of the Universe, and even as ultimate reality or Brahman.

We could get lost in tracing Erotic-monster-makers across cultures and time, but as my friend and author Sophie Strand often says, we might summarily exclaim, all monster myths are mother myths. And what we observe in even these few examples is a correlation between the monstrous chaos and the generativity of making; between the terror of unknowing and the creative act; between the erotic flame and the fluid, penetrable, feminine conceptual possibility.

Eros's longing has always troubled us. It disrupts the clean categories and rational order. It seems birthed in chaos and often leaves destruction in its wake. It is the monster in the unknown beyond our lines and the one hidden deep within. The calamitous desire we have been taught to fear, to tame.

These myths demand we reckon with what scares us the most about walking into the uncertain future beyond the safety of our enclosures. The monstrous-maker in life itself is its inherent unknowability, its messiness, its nonbinary queerness, its refusal to be contained. The rift that yawns open like the mouth of a great monster in our moment of ecological reckoning forces us to look into the darkest depths at how we handle what frightens us about life . . . what is uncontrollable, what we cannot predict or know.

The ancients, in their fear of Eros, properly reverenced it as an elemental force. Creativity *is* scary. It is the godding power to unmake and make—not just artistically or even biologically but socially in relationships, perspectives, and beliefs. And such power can be all-consuming, can possess us in the throes of its longing intensity, overthrow the rational order of certitudes, identities, and even kingdoms, aka institutions, and take us into the unknown.

My fascination with Eros is how desire drives human imagination and creativity. The aim of our desire, in a way, creates us. Which is why understanding its power, and increasing our mindfulness about how we employ our imagination, is so urgently vital. Instead of strengthening our capacity to imagine better or new possibilities, most of our desire is hijacked in guarding against the uncertainty of change. Our human instinctual response to the existential terror of uncertainty is predominantly one of control, domination, or colonizing the unknown. When I consider my response to the unknown in my own life, creatively, relationally, or circumstantially, I can compassionately understand and witness how fear drives the impulse to control or dominate. That's what I was taught to do.

The internalized dominance of being a "good girl" my entire life played into these rules of control, perhaps especially those rules of spiritual equations. X+Y=Salvation. I believed that if I just followed the order of rationality, of my spiritual maps and beliefs (inherited narratives keeping wild, monstrous terror of the unknown at bay), that I would be rewarded with a safe "arrival" and be "complete." But Eros refuses the half-life of such order, and she ripped into my map and my life and left a gaping rift through which I would be reborn.

For some time, my then-husband and I had been scotch-taping our marriage. I was forever drawn to asking the questions, to the creative risk, to the mystical edges of religion, while he was more comfortable in the known, in traditional religion, and in the expected shapes of life prescribed by institution. Our sons were six and three when we decided to take a trip to Scotland, tacked onto a work trip he had. We planned to meet up with his boss in London, and when we arrived, mysteriously and suddenly violently ill, my husband insisted I go to dinner with his boss without him, an unremarkably normal request akin to taking the trash out or picking up some groceries. That night, however, was anything but normal.

His boss was full of questions about my mystical studies, about my favorite mystic—Teilhard de Chardin—whose work I focused on for the equivalent of a graduate thesis at the time. He was inquisitive, thoughtful, curious. The last thing I remember clearly is the glass of wine before me. The rest of my memories are snippets of a nightmare: my head hitting a wall. A belt buckle pressing into my stomach. The roughness of his beard on my neck. Not being able to stand.

And whatever narrative my mind tried to puzzle together from the confused snippets of nonlinear memories, it still resisted the worst conclusions. It wasn't until he chillingly and calmly told me himself the next day what had happened, which in his words were "I knew you needed to cut loose, so I helped you out a little," that the horror became real. A bomb went off, and I curved around the shrapnel as though I could stop it from hitting everyone else I loved, and the sharp edges of a scream lodged frozen in my throat.

When the scream finally wrenched free, and I came forward about what had happened, it was as if that shrapnel exited my body only to turn back around and hit me again. Because this was prior to the #MeToo movement, I suffered the worst classic victim shaming and he-said/she-said dismissal from the Christian organization he and my then-husband worked for. A criminal lawsuit wasn't an option since it happened overseas, and I didn't have the capacity in my traumatized state for a civil lawsuit.

Eventually, other women came forward. Eventually, that man was fired . . . with a hefty severance package and nondisclosures so that the organization could never reveal what had happened, that is.

Eventually, my then-husband went back to work and was told to make sure I kept my mouth shut about what happened, to make sure I *stayed inside the lines*. Eventually, things went back to "normal" . . . for everyone else but me.

I was sleeping on the floor of our tiny guest bedroom because, for some reason, sleeping in a small, enclosed place and on the hard surface of the floor was the only solidity that kept me from waking countless times throughout the night in a cold sweat with that scream in my throat. I couldn't smell cologne or see men's dress shoes or belt buckles without having a panic attack. It was years before I could handle being in an airport surrounded by businessmen without hiding in the bathroom stalls in a fetal position.

And every day that my then-husband came home from working for the people who didn't believe me and later told him to make sure I kept my mouth shut, I got smaller and smaller. Quieter and quieter. The lines of enclosure around me got tighter and tighter until they choked me like a noose. Until I couldn't breathe. And it almost killed me.

Some marriages might have weathered that storm.

I remember how, around that time, an old apple tree in our backyard suddenly just toppled to the ground one windless, stormless day. When we went to look at it, we discovered that half of it was rotted inside. It could have stood for another decade, maybe two, and no one would have known. But it fell. It just . . . *fell.*

Who knows why things happen the way they do? Why the tree fell that day and not any other? Why or how it had been living and rotting at the same time? Is it any less real for having lived as it died? And is my marriage any less real for having created in its life, even though it died too? Do my wild and wonderful sons not stand as proof of that mingling, middling reality?

My life as I knew it ended. All the neat edges, borders, and softly colored maps in the world could not rescue me from tragedy. The lines shattered, and in the fragments of what I thought my life was going to be, a new life shape emerged.

I'm not excusing sociopathic behavior or violence. But here's what I will say: in the months and years of therapy that ensued, I developed a new relationship with my traumatized body and through it became related to any and all bodies whose power of agency has ever been taken away. I became membered to a much larger human and more-than-human experience, and because of it, a different kind of understanding about myself in membership to all bodies emerged.

In the slow years of healing after my divorce, I remembered bits of me that I had nearly lost. The parts that knew how to move without permission . . . how to color *outside* the lines, how to dance, how to sing. And I pieced myself together, sharp edge next to sharp colorful edge, until I became a riot of unexpected edges, a vivid collage of more than one thing.

The girl I was before died. Everything I thought I knew died. Someone else rose from that grave. Someone who not only had to reckon with unknowing but who was no longer afraid of not knowing.

Four years later, the world was baptized into a collective unknowing with the pandemic. And once again—this time as a single working mom—I faced that tear in the matrix of our expectations of business as usual. The Washington, DC organization I was working for lost its funding, and I was suddenly without a job amid a global pandemic.

I remember feeling the urge to cling to the familiar, to just run and go get another job as a creative for someone else's vision. *Stay inside the lines*, the voices said. But something deep in me stilled. I turned to that monstrous shape-shifter, to that hideous godding Eros caged inside me, and on the edge of the cliff I stood on in my life, I heard it whisper the gauntlet of creative challenge, "*What if?*" I looked at my two kids, these miraculous, magical creatures, and thought about the values I wanted to exemplify for them and leave them as my legacy: courage, creativity, and compassion. So I decided it was now or never, and I leapt: I centered the creative expressions of my life in a total about-face back to being a maker.

I started a podcast called *Unknowing*. I wrote and recorded an entire album. I began painting again. I dared to believe that maybe, just maybe, coloring outside the lines, leaving the maps behind, and *unknowing* weren't just ideas but the entire path and praxis of being a maker in this world.

Surely you've felt it.

Just below the surface of your everyday life, the monster-maker crouches behind the lines of your too-small shapes, whispering the question, "*What if you didn't have to color inside the lines of life-as-it-has-been-prescribed?*" Eros's fire incinerates the moments of recognition and achievement you thought would sate you, leaving an ashy taste in your mouth as you ask yourself, "*If this was really the goal, then why don't I feel more satisfied?*" Eros catches you in her web when you've been shattered by tragedy and gently spins your fragments into a new shape. Eros expands like roots beneath you in your quietest moments in nature and seductively pulls you beneath the surface of your life, giving you an ecstatic glimpse of connectedness with all pulsing, throbbing life around you, from the startling flash of the blue jay overhead to the whispered sigh of the breeze in the grasses.

Eros is the inspiration the body exhales upon touching on a too-full feeling of fulfillment that the rational mind quickly brushes aside in your hurry to get back to the rationalized order of "business as usual." Eros retreats and diminishes as we endlessly scroll on our feeds, in direct proportion to our distracted retreating from our potential, and as we cleverly disguise such diminishment as "entertainment." Eros sings like a siren in the star-filled night-horizons beyond your sight, animating some ancient instinct in you to move beyond familiar places and spaces when the air grows stale, when the oxygen leaves the institution, building, or relationship.

It's almost as if life refuses to be contained too long, no matter how good, sweet, or helpful the womb is. The shapes shift, the circle opens, and life always moves through the disruptions, breaks, and spaces between lines. The edges of your broken heart become the site of your own rebirth.

Our hearts break not only because of tragedy but occasionally from beauty too. Can't you feel your heart crack open when you think of that one time you felt held by the trees in the woods, the sunrise after you became a father, the way your lover's body seems to perfectly fit and tuck around yours? And because the piercing of the heart is Eros's language, art, the imaginal, possible, and moreness of what-could-be are her temples. Which is why we automatically speak in hushed, whispered tones of reverence in a museum. Why we gather like congregants at a concert. Why we read poetic litanies like prayer.

A burning ache in your chest that is set aflame when you listen to Thom York's quivering voice soar in a way that makes your soul tremble. A curl in your stomach that drops when you stand before a Basquiat, your eyes roving the colors as if touching and being touched by them, feeling the passionate strokes he made on the canvas on your own body like a ravenous lover's caress.

A moment of homecoming before a Picasso, of seeing someone paint something you had felt deep within you in a way that grants you permission to imagine your life beyond the expected shapes of what has been.

And even when the worst comes to pass, and you find yourself split open and shattered by tragedy or grief, you hear Eros's voice urging you to not give up, to keep going—in the poetic lines in David Whyte's poem "Sweet Darkness":

The dark will be your home
tonight.

The night will give you a horizon
further than you can see.

You must learn one thing.
The world was made to be free in.

Give up all the other worlds
except the one to which you belong.

Sometimes it takes darkness and the sweet
confinement of your aloneness
to learn

anything or anyone
that does not bring you alive

is too small for you.

Eros's unknowability calls to our tame lives because something in us recognizes that having this nice, controlled, predictable, "safe" life is, indeed, too small. In the ache we feel is the recognition that we have forgotten who and what we are . . . that we are makers, not consumers of a prescribed life. That we've settled for scripted lives and playing the parts handed to us. Eros awakens the wild-maker, with its monstrous unknown contours, because as part of this thrumming, throbbing, teeming cosmos of life seeking more life, a greater *moreness* calls to you beyond, "further than you can see."

As the dynamism of change, Eros is the "tyrant of the gods." And because of that—assign any term you prefer to this life-force—this Love is bigger than any categories: The ashes we are born from when the life we thought we knew goes up in flames. The precipice we leap off of when we begin all new endeavors. The fall we make when we fall in love. The desire to give up one world with the aid of another, to die to what has been for the sake of what could be.

Life is not afraid of death, nor does life see death as some sort of dualistic nemesis. Life embraces death because any block, ending, or limitation is worked with and through to new ends. "Only because of death does life become creative," says Weber. This is not a romanticization of death but rather a biological reality: even the dead house life in their composting/decay. Understanding metabolization as one life ending in one form and being converted to energy in another changes everything.

When I consider every death in my own life, every institution I belonged to that I outgrew, every garden I eventually flew out of like Lilith in my hunger to freely exist and be liberated to create, every tragedy, every death of a loved one or relationship . . . the direction of my life seems to be stubbornly bent toward *more*. My life, through every death, has become more alive.

So let me ask you, then, what world is calling you to let go of the one you know? What heart-tug can you no longer ignore, distract yourself from, or deny? Eros stands in the threshold between now and "might-be," between what has been and the possibility of what could be. Eros is the herald of transformation. And really, that is perhaps the most frightening thing of all. Because change requires us to let go of what we know and what is familiar.

Meanwhile, the unknown beckons, like a lover awaiting our willingness to risk our hearts and gain the world. Meanwhile Eros awaits your courage to imagine more and *make* something brave with the shape of your life.

Chapter Three

A Secret Seduction
The Allure of an Unknowing Imagination

> *Leave the door open for the unknown, the door into the dark. That's where the most important things come from, where you yourself came from, and where you will go.*
>
> —Rebecca Solnit

No less than six medical students sat in the room looking bored and no doubt hoping I would fail so some real excitement would begin. I was eleven hours into labor with my second son, Rowan, with whom I was attempting a VBAC (vaginal birth after the cesarean of my first), and in that moment, I wasn't sure what would happen first: the birth of my baby or the murder I was about to commit of the disinterested med students.

Another contraction. I ripped off the hospital gown, not caring that I was now fully naked before the peanut gallery before me . . . slick with sweat and no doubt looking like a primordial goddess of birth and destruction. Yes, birth and destruction were very much on the agenda.

Another contraction. One of the med students wouldn't stop clicking his pen as he watched the Netflix show that was my cervix.

"CAN SOMEONE PLEASE GET THE CHILD DOCTOR A CRAYON?" The bored students looked up. Oops, I yelled that out loud, not just in my head. Oh w . . . fuck, another contraction. Someone—a nurse? A saintly apparition? My imagination?—said, "Okay, honey, it's time to push." At last, a productive purpose to which I could direct my rage and hope. Wave upon wave of contraction came, and with each I did my best to ride the crest and push with everything I had.

"He's cresting!" yelled one of the students, looking up at me with wonder. Ah, so natural births could be exciting to them after all . . . imagine that. I reached down and felt the head of my son between my legs. It was 110 percent as weird as it sounds.

"Just a couple more pushes," said my then-husband next to me, whom, let's be clear . . . I also felt murderous toward. At that point it wasn't personal, just a general global homicidal outlook toward all but the little being I was trying to deliver.

Two pushes and three lifetimes later, a tiny and very loud slippery body emerged from my swollen and exhausted one, and I held him for the first time. He was an angel-alien. Huge gray-blue, wide, blinking eyes looked at me, and I forgot my own name and anything that had ever existed before that moment. And then I looked up and through tears saw the most miraculous sight: six med students, one then-husband, and two nurses crowded around, their faces transfigured with light . . . absolute awe on their faces. A few even had tears in their eyes.

My then-husband's emotion made sense, but what got me was witnessing the others. Despite all the things those med students and nurses thought they knew, and despite all the many other experiences they may have witnessed, life still surprised them with the miraculous, raw, messy immediacy of unforeseen beauty.

Imagine that.

I didn't know what would happen. I couldn't have predicted whether a vaginal birth would work or if I'd need another cesarean. Any mother knows that primal terror that comes over you as you reckon with all that *could* go wrong in a birth. When we give birth, we have one foot in life and one in death, and we are brought to our knees in reverencing both in the unknowing.

Uncertainty is the preamble to possibility. It is only in being uncertain that we are capable of the humility of suspending our expectations, our assumptions, our cemented beliefs poured like concrete over the greening, living potential. Without a doubt, what frightens us most about life is the unknown. It's scary because we immediately assume the worst might or will happen. Evolutionarily, being prepared for the worst was the difference between escaping the attack of the saber-tooth tiger or becoming its snack. What is truly scary, however, is how our fear of the unknown can cause us to retreat to the safe enclosure of certitudes, preferencing what is familiar, predictable, and known. The more we do this, the less life has room to expand, create the unexpected, or surprise us with beauty. Uncertainty is the beginning of reckoning with humor at how much we don't know, the relief of our ignorance that leads to unthreatened curiosity and creativity.

In life, in creativity, we have to let go of what we think we know to make room for what could be. This is the half-hidden garden gate to everything we dream of: our willingness to surrender our tired stories, our worn concrete paths, our too-tight shoes someone else told us to wear and instead step barefoot into a moss-cushioned, dark forest of may-be and might-be. It is the stuff of the fairy tales we grew up with, the landscape of inspired ingenuity found by every great author, thinker, maker who has ever walked this earth. The creative act of life is, in the words attributed to Mary Magdalene, *leaving one world with the aid of another.*

Because life is creative, it only moves in one direction: toward more life . . . even through death and dying. Life will let go of what-has-been to engender what-could-be. As life, love, creativity are all interchangeable in our understanding of Eros, you can assume that if you want to live life fully alive, love with abandon, or be deeply generative, you're going to have to move through the discomfort of facing the unknown, of letting go of what has been, again and again and again. You are going to have to shift your relationship to the unknown. You are going to have to learn to not only tolerate but befriend unknowing.

The first way we do this is by making peace with what we cannot see in the darkness. Not imagining the darkness holds a threatening monster but a loving, dark, womblike embrace of everything that is waiting to be made real in and through you.

Think about every beautiful, amazing, wonderful surprise that's ever happened in your life. Did they not also, at one point, emerge from the unknown? What if the Unknown (any and all unknown circumstances you are currently facing) is inviting you to expand by surrendering your pessimism, self-assured certitudes, and scripts of everything you think you know? What might happen if you shifted into seeing the Unknown as a more benevolent presence, as the open-endedness of a more loving—and therefore creative—imagination?

I can practically hear you thinking, "But, Brie, it's precisely my very creative imagination that conjures up the worst possibilities of what could happen." I get it! My ex-husband, with whom I still share a thriving and loving co-parenting relationship, will often quote Mark Twain to the kids and me when any of us gets anxious or worries: "I have suffered a great many catastrophes in my life, most of which never occurred." Trust me, I know how quickly our minds can conjure up terrible things to be afraid of.

It is in fact true, as we just explored, that sometimes the earth you are standing on shifts in a terrifying earthquake. And everything you thought you knew crumbles through tragedy, grief, or loss. It's not that tragic catastrophes don't happen.

But I happen to believe that if all we do is fear the catastrophic, our lives will be catastrophically wasted, and the true tragedy will be missing the creative potential we know in our souls we were meant for.

Notice I said that perhaps the Unknown is inviting you to have a *more benevolent . . . and therefore creative* imagination. In the birthing story of Rowan, I could have easily surrendered to the pessimism in the room that I wasn't going to be able to healthily deliver my son after a C-section. I could have totally given into the fear and asked them to take me to surgery (and that would have been okay, by the way; I'm not making a declarative judgment on how babies are born). But my choice was to hang on to the belief that I *could* deliver him vaginally; I held on to a faith in my body's creative power to do so. And I made that choice with my whole heart. It could have been beyond my control and had his heart rate started plummeting, I would have gladly done what was needed. My point is that I first needed to *believe* it was possible in order to even have the courage to try. Only the choice to accept the invitation to the unknown allowed me to prove those bored medical students wrong.

My faith-as-imagination also helped me rise from the ashes of tragedy, create possibilities I couldn't have predicted, and become the woman I am becoming. I'm fascinated by how in the Christian Gospels Jesus is quoted as saying, "Your faith has healed you." Perhaps he wasn't crediting people's faith in Jesus as the miracle but, rather, their faith in themselves to become something new.

Shifting into a creative trust in the Unknown—instead of terror—is the difference between being blindfolded by a trusted lover and not seeing through a thick fog you are driving into. In both scenarios, you cannot see. In the first, however, we are totally surrendered to the ways our other senses of touch, smell, taste are opened up, and our entire orientation is one of anticipation, pleasure, and relaxed trust. In the second, you're obviously praying to all the gods, sweating bullets, swearing in every language, white-knuckling the wheel, totally terrified.

Which version of not-seeing sounds more pleasurable? More enlivening? And if it were just as easy as yelling, "Blindfolded-lover life, I choose fifty shades of living!" into the night sky, then there would be no point in my writing this book. Learning how to shift from that second mindset to the first when facing the Unknown takes practice.

The first step begins with owning that you *are indeed* actively choosing a core narrative to fuel your beliefs and therefore the shape of your life. What you believe matters (becomes mattered and real). As Richard Rohr says, "Your image of God creates you." The image you hold of what is ultimately real—creates you. Our imaginations are powerful, dangerous conduits that create something out of nothing. What it is you cocreate depends largely on your choice. Will you conjure fear with all the hate, terror, and smallness fear creates? Or will you conjure love, enlivenment, expansion, and pleasurable possibility?

To tap into that creative power requires first learning how to drop beneath the mind's automatic terror-conjuring and instead choosing a more positive and therefore creative imagination. Most of us operate within this AI (anxious interpretation) mind of our reactive thoughts constantly scrolling like a fear-feed. We are so busy walking around with our heads down staring at that AI mind-feed that it's no wonder we are constantly running into each other, getting stuck, or walking into a wall. We are on autopilot, making choices and stories entirely conjured by our own limited beliefs, narratives, and interpretations. Living this way puts us in constant reaction, not creation.

The only moment with creative power is the present moment.

This is the only moment when what you believe meets reality in the mingling of making beliefs real. The only place where creativity happens is now.

In his famous poem "Go to the Limits of Your Longing," the poet Rainer Maria Rilke declares this present-moment cocreating we are actively engaged in with God as being contingent on our willingness to bear the limits of our longing. To feel everything, *we have to be embodied and present.*

So how do we fully meet that creative power?

The body is the vessel for presence. You cannot think your way into presence. Presence is an embodied blooming of sensation, an opening up of your senses—noticing your breath, what you feel, what you hear—so that the rest of you can come online. For me, presence is an activation similar to arousal, shifting out of letting my thoughts dictate what matters to letting more of me matter than just my thoughts. Then, from that place of seductively embodied presence, I choose.

For a longtime, I had unknowingly been practicing this radical embodied presence and faith-as-imagination because all creativity is born from this kind of full-bodied presence.

The first time I tried meditation, I was in my twenties at a spiritual conference on mysticism. I was trying to follow the prompts by the person guiding it, but I was nervous. *Am I doing this right?* I thought. And then, *Shit, I'm supposed to let go of my thoughts.* I tried coming back to my breath, but, strangely, the more focused I was on my breath, the more I started to feel like I wasn't breathing right. It was a hilarious crash course in the hall of mirrors of my own mind. After about fifteen minutes, my mind began to settle; my awareness began to still and dropped to a deeper place within me. My breath became more rhythmic, and my body became more enlivened, more fully aware . . . without getting hooked in a story going on in my mind.

As I began to drop into this depth, a felt sense muscle memory and recognition came: *I know this place.* The sensory, fluid, nonnarrative, embodied presence that meditation touches upon is the same place artists create from, in glimpses of that larger (re)membered, nonidentified presence. This was the same place I had been going to for years when I wrote songs . . . the same place I go from which I "catch" melodies out of the ether. The same place I paint from when I channel images . . . impressions. The place I used to drop into when dancing. It's the place where my "mind" (thoughts, ideas, expectations, projections) no longer runs the show. Instead, I'm in a surrendered posture of embodied listening and receiving, a wordless and thoughtless seeking and expressing . . . the utter seductive flow of becoming a vessel for love as it shapes itself through me. In this place, I drop into a self that is here-and-arriving, a personhood that is both me but also not-me or *more-than-me*.

It's the very same place lovers go in the thrall of lovemaking . . . when instead of mind-over-matter, more matters than the mind. When I am making love, I'm fully surrendered in the act of touch and touching, giving and receiving pleasure; the body opens to an expanded sensual presence and single-hearted focus. Entangled with a lover, we are sated in the present moment *and* hungering for more in the mounting coming ecstasy.

It's also the place we all touch upon in moments of great beauty, love, and wonder. Or what grief opens us up to in our suffering, losses, and tragedies. It's where and how your heart breaks because the breaking signifies another self-enclosed protection that you are breaking out of. The veil of our tiny, egoic identities parts, allowing us to glimpse the shared immensity of our unknowable shared becoming. Our hearts ache as they stretch with vulnerable tenderness to make room for the *moreness* of such an expansion. The bittersweet ache of longing lingers when you realize that you don't know anything at all. The yearning that tugs at your heart, fills you with wonder, and lights you up yields into a desire to serve such immensity.

Learning how to meditate and implicitly understanding it not as some transcendental badge of arrival but as strengthening the creative muscle was a natural connection for me. Meditation isn't the only way to strengthen this muscle, for it is strengthened in you every time you practice giving yourself away in a way that enlivens you as you enliven others. We do, however, all need *some* kind of way to intentionally and regularly practice this kind of embodied presence, or the mind will keep doing its AI programming thing.

Embodied presence is not only the portal to the creative power of choosing our mindset, choosing to befriend the Unknown, but it's also the portal to everything we *need:* resilience, hope, energy, abundance, courage. In every exhausted moment I've faced as a mom that I've stopped enough to let my mind drop into my body and come online through sensation, I feel like I am growing taproots. These roots reach the wellspring of a sense of humor, a dose of wonder. Every moment I surrender what I think I know and stand fully in my body before a canvas or my instruments, a surge of inspiration rises beneath me in a playful push of possibility. Every moment I choose to be fully disrobed in vulnerability before a lover, figuratively or literally, the power of tenderness allures and elicits more love than I could ever imagine or exhaust.

That kind of liberated power can only be found *when you can consciously choose it.* You will not find it when your AI mind runs the fear-feed and you are in perpetual reaction. More than ever, the world desperately needs creatives ruthless in their originality, authentic voice, and freedom to embody ways that increase our mutual connectedness, enlivenment and animate our creativity.

Imagination is the realm from which the creative is ushering an "image" or idea into manifestation, connecting a thread that draws magic from the future potential "could be" into the reality of the present here and now. But another way the AI mind hijacks us from that connected thread is through fantasy. Fantasy, in contrast, is the *escape from the reality of the here and now* into an imagined alternative *without any intention to concretely create or manifest it in your life.* In so doing, fantasy holds our creativity hostage. All that creative energy is held captive to sustain this escape route rather than being channeled into the real tangible work of making art, manifesting ideas or concrete changes *in reality.*

This is something I run into a lot with creatives who tell me they have millions of ideas but never can actually start anything. In part, this is because it's much safer to fantasize about all the things you could create than to courageously and vulnerably work to bring the *image-in* to reality. Fantasy perpetuates stasis. Imagination demands brave creation. And if you don't serve creation, the "muscle" or the capacity for it will atrophy. Conversely, the more you bring the image-in via your willingness to create and make it real, the more your imagination will increase.

Witnessing the AI fear-feed of your mind will tell you everything you need to know about the state of your heart and your erotic-creative life-force. Is your mind-scroll full of constant comparisons? Are you busy judging others to try to make yourself feel better than? Are you hooked on negativity and worry? Are you obsessed with proving your worth via achievements or success? Answering yes to any of those questions likely means you are struggling to create with abandon, anxiously allowing your insecurity to impact your relationships, or teetering on the edge of exhaustion and burnout.

As artists and lovers, creating and loving from a place of calm, embodied confidence is key. We do not experience confidence that what we are making will be well received but rather that we are enough to serve the making now. Our creativity is the risk taken *here and now* in brave vulnerability of tenderness by willingly sharing ourselves, in vulnerably letting others in, in letting ourselves touch and be touched through our offerings. It is an embodied, present practice of enlivenment as we enliven.

If you are caught up in your insecurities, you're going to have a hard time ripping your clothes off and passionately loving with abandon. Similarly, you cannot create greatly from a place hemmed in by comparison or fear. True creativity is only possible when your sense of worth is rooted in something deeper than the AI-mind external validation points.

Your entire identity as an erotic-creative needs to shift from the small personal dramas of the fragile, insecure "I" into selfhood that is larger and can never be defined or determined by anything that has happened or may happen to you. Trading the tiny, static identity for the power of who you really are: a mystery and miracle of life on its way to becoming *more.*

You are not your job. You are not your marital status or decision to have children or not. You are not your future accomplishments. And you are certainly not your past.

Two days after the worst happened to me on that fateful trip, I remember how my body, to protect me, completely and utterly shut down and went numb. And how my mind, again to protect me, became completely disassociated. For three days after the assault, I was a corpse. I walked, talked, and moved. I did everything I could to not believe that the unthinkable had indeed happened. Every time my then-husband went to the bathroom, his boss verbally and physically harassed me as we continued traveling with him for three days after what happened in London. I would freeze and turn to stone. I was dead inside. I was a ghost. During the day, I walked and walked and walked, for hours and miles . . . never even registering my blistered feet. I felt nothing.

On the third day in Amsterdam, I walked the city aimlessly . . . with no plan except to keep walking, perhaps just to prove to myself that by walking, being in motion, I was still alive. I had Little Dragon blaring in my ears, and when the album ended, I was surprised to find myself in front of the Stedelijk Museum. They had an exhibit of one of my favorite artists whose work I saw countless times in my childhood in Europe: the incomparable Matisse.

As I walked through the museum and stood before familiar painting after familiar painting, I had the distinct impression that Matisse was looking at me as I was looking at him, painting by painting. In the final room was an exhibit of the priestly robes he designed to go in the chapel he designed, the Chapelle du Rosaire de Vence, and in the glass protecting the dark black and white contrast of one such robe, I saw my own reflection. My eyes hollowed, my face gaunt. I looked like a dead person. But then, and I cannot explain it any other way, I felt Matisse say to me, "*This is not who you are.*" And in that moment, I suddenly saw myself before that same Matisse piece as a child of five, seven, ten, twelve, as if he had remembered me standing before his work each of those times and was playing it all back to me like a videotape to remind me.

There I was staring up at him with pigtails. There I was, elsewhere in Europe . . . a different setting, a few inches taller, my brown eyes huge and stark against my little pale face and blond hair. There I was at ten, somewhere else . . . still looking up at him. And at twelve, now in the States, prepubescent, looking lost and awkwardly out of place. My eyes a little shier now, a little more self-conscious.

Then the tape sped up. I saw myself older, and older still, until I was before him as an old woman . . . with two different-colored socks, wearing some fabulous vintage dress and fur coat, and not giving a damn (because this is how I imagine I will look in my old age) in a future impression of myself standing before those same pieces in my future life.

And then the tape sped up even more, impossibly fast blinks of impressions of every face, body, person that had ever stood before this Matisse. And through this moment of being touched by this piece, were they not also part of the strange magic that was now touching me and healing me?

Matisse played my life back to me as he saw it. And it was as if in showing me these images, he helped me become (re)membered to a self beyond what had happened, that would never be defined by the horror of what had been done to me. A self not bound by time, a self that lives on mycelially and eternally . . . because it was a self that was larger than any enclosed, temporal, fixed identity.

Matisse helped me unknow what I thought would define me forever so that I could continue becoming *more.*

A sob wrenched free in me. For the first time in three days, I could feel again. This feeling-ness did not happen in my mind. It was not an idea. This feeling was somatically embodied. I felt it experientially as a thawing of my senses returning me to the land of the living.

My body began to shake as I wept before that sacred robe made by the artist who in his own life was no stranger to suffering. And as the tears fell, I felt myself come back to life.

My healing would take years, but in that moment, I was no longer a corpse. On that third day, I was resurrected. Matisse brought me back to life.

Sometimes we are violently stripped of everything we think we are . . . and inexplicably, without justifying such violence, in the lowest moments, we are (re)membered to the self that can never be imprisoned in the tragedy of what happens to us.

Sometimes we die before we die so that we can taste how love and life flow through death to another life beyond it. We are so much more than these identities, these tiny little fixed symbols of notes on the staff, lines of a page. We are the song of the universe, only perceptible by the symphonic music pouring through us as the instrument of our bodies resounds in the unfolding song of life.

The secret seduction of alluring our imagination is found in ways we willingly let more Love, more Life, and a more erotic-creative practice *in.* Unknowing is the ultimate alluring lover, half-hidden in the shadows, gazing at us with a seductive dare. Occasionally, unknowing teases us with a glimpse of our larger potential, a little flirtatious sneak-peak into what could be. But the only moment when unknowing meets us in the embrace of creating new life and new possibility with us is this one. If you are present and not too distracted, that is.

Chapter Four

(be)Coming Together
The Process Is the Product

Art is not a thing, it is a way.

—Elbert Hubbard

Wait for the day,
come early or late.

I sang the words of my song into the microphone to sound check, sitting at the bottom of an elevator shaft in complete darkness at three in the morning. Like you do.

Time . . . she makes it worth it . . .
But time is hard to take.

Jay patched in, "Can you hear me?"

"Yup," I answered, suppressing a yawn.

"Okay, keep singing. We're going to dial in the plate reverb a little more."

Wait for the day,
Come early or late.
And if you should doubt . . .
She'll come, anyway.

"Hi." Jay walked in through the service door.

I nearly jumped out of my skin. "Holy shit, Jay!"

"Are you awake now?" he chuckled in his low, gravely baritone as he adjusted my microphone.

"I am arriving momentarily," my disoriented brain translated from the Spanish *ya llego.*

"The gerund," he said, "—or is it an infinitive?—makes more sense there actually . . . you are, and you are arriving, and it's a moment-by-moment process." He fiddled with one of the many cables that hung like snakes down the elevator shaft as he talked.

At three in the morning, he lost me with one of his typical philosophical meanderings. We were in the Pieholden studio, essentially a giant warehouse in Chicago. I was twenty-one years old when I was dropped off there with my friend David Vandervelde to record with the famed multi-instrumentalist Jay Bennet. Jay had just left the band Wilco and was taking on projects as a producer. I remember when I drove down with a member of the label I was signed with to meet him for the first time. His manager welcomed us in, woke up Jay, and moments later, he emerged from the control room with pants held up by a string, duct tape on one shoe, two different socks, hair like Einstein, and somehow simultaneously holding in his right hand a coffee cup, a cigarette, and a cookie.

He was a mad scientist, a genius of musical experimentation. He was too brilliant for this world. I wish he was still with us. Jay left me in the elevator shaft and then came back in, carrying a various assortment of things under his arm. He had a few random kitschy scarves that he began draping around the small space and some old saint candles he started lighting.

"Why do you do that? Why do you always make it pretty?" I asked him, still half asleep.

He kept up his mood-making as he answered over his shoulder, his voice deep as the ocean and gravely as the sediment at its floor, "Well, my dear, because it will impact you . . . because you will feel it, so it will come out in your voice, and then, through you, whoever listens to you will feel it too." He stopped for a minute and turned toward me. "Because, darlin', the process is the product." He winked.

It was Jay's fundamental principle in recording. He said it all the time. Everything was part of the record we were making. The warehouse wasn't just a studio, it was a player. And we harmonized with it by experimenting with its contours, recording all over the building: in the hall, in the stairwell. We created "garbage" drum kits by duct taping things to the actual drum kit—chairs, boxes, even broken glass on the snare— and let it all echo through the room, creating its own unique shape of delay.

Perfection was not the goal; playfulness and experimentation were. We recorded on two-inch tape, which was a luxury and an analogue dream in a time when music had gone totally digital. So there was no auto-tuning, no digital manipulation. The imperfect process and embracing "mistakes" became the vulnerable bridges of connection by touching the listener. And whatever we made together, there was a recognition that it was all bigger than the tiny melodies I had birthed with my '69 acoustic Gibson Hummingbird.

Jay was my first producer, and while I didn't realize it at the time, the lessons I learned from him formed an entire creative philosophical orientation in my life. He liked waking me up to track vocals when I wasn't expecting it. It was never a controlling or demanding energy but rather a playful and curious, almost childlike, trickster energy that was infectious. In this case, he said he wanted to know what my vocals would sound like when I was "not prepared," and when I was alone in the dark, in the belly of the beast of the building at the bottom of the elevator shaft.

To be an artist is to choose back the discomfort, choose the uncertainty of being willing to experiment because that

Unknowing is what keeps us close to the tenderness of vulnerability. And we make from that place. And we become willing to touch on how staying open, unsure, is necessary to the creative process and the hardest part. That same courageous willingness is what also helps us realize that pleasure, joy, wonder are not relegated to the end, to an outcome, but rather can be conjured and woven into every step of the way. Like Jay said, when the process feels good—is full of beauty, wonder, intentionality—the outcome will be good, beautiful, wonderful, intentional. The process is the product.

Imagine for a moment how different my experience in the studio could have been if fear and control ran the show. I would have been entirely focused on the time each experiment took and would have been in a scarcity-mindset about the amount of work we had to do, measured against the days the studio was booked. I doubt I would have been down to be woken up at all hours or placed at the bottom of an elevator shaft. The atmosphere in the studio would have gone from one of trust and collaborative, playful creativity (erotically enlivened) to one of control, sucking all the life and possibilities out with it.

Jay experimented playfully with the confidence of someone who was not at all insecure or afraid of mistakes. He trusted his gut. He was fully in the moment, totally unhurried, embodied, and in touch with his instincts. Because of that playful freedom, he was incredibly prolific. One of the founders of my current record label, Bill Hein, recently told me a story of when he had signed Jay to Rykodisc. They asked Jay to turn in his top, paired-down-to-the-best material. Jay handed over twenty CDs full of demos. It's not that he misunderstood the directive but rather that he had picked twenty CDs out of a hundred.

The ability to create more (love, life, art) will increase as you are less caught up in feeding, protecting, and projecting your insecurities. The willingness to experiment in playful relational curiosity, to not identify with what we are doing, to be open to the unknown . . . these are essential practices of the erotic creative. But *how do we do it?* How do we make a shift from insecurity to confidence? From closed off and controlling to playful and creative? How do we make the process of creating *feel* as good as we hope the outcome will be?

Sex is a great illustration of how the process is the product. Sure, climax shimmers on the horizon of your awareness. You know it, and your partner knows it, and you're both (hopefully) intent on arousing and serving each other's pleasure, seeking the release in the other. But the nature of the mounting orgasmic pleasure is both a "here" and "coming" reality. The more you are fully savoring the embodied luscious "here," the more shattering the "coming" is.

Likewise, the way you think of yourself in the flux of lovemaking is both a distinct "you," but also—entangled literally and figuratively in the thrall of your lover—you are a "more-than-you." You are a *we*. And that *togetherness* gives you a certain supported freedom to move beyond your insecurities and love with abandon.

So it seems that the spell needed in making the process as playful and pleasurable as the product has something to do with shifting from a "me" to a "we" and in holding a simultaneity of understanding yourself as both here and coming . . . in other words, as *in process yourself*.

Jay, in his creativity, exemplified this lived poetic stance. He was fully in the moment, not insecure and fragile, *because* he was so deeply collaborative (his "me" was shifted to a "we") and he held the never-finished, never-arrived posture of one who believed they could always keep learning, growing, expressing as an artist.

This way of being represents a radical shift in how we typically think of ourselves. In philosophy, this is an *ontological* shift (ontology, the exploration of the nature of being). It's worth naming that how we see ourselves is largely influenced by inherited philosophical categories and ideas, many of which are woefully out of date with what science is telling us about the nature of the universe. But we cling to them anyway. Why? Well, because it's familiar.

Centuries of dualisms—beginning way back with Plato's soul or mind/body split and reified by Descartes—have kept us enamored with the mind and dismissive of the body. We perpetuate a Newtonian worldview (long since transcended scientifically) when we continue to think of the world and the universe as machinelike and reducible to tiny, separate building-block bits. Even though science has corrected this view, we still tend to view people in the same way—as separate Legos: fixed "identities" only made clear by understanding how they stand apart. Which one of these is not like the other? A circle is a circle because it is not a square. I am *me* because I am NOT you.

These perspectives have kept us locked into believing that our personhood is (1) defined by our thoughts and minds (thanks, Descartes); (2) a static, fully finished "I am"; and (3) separate and isolated from everyone else. Essentially, the opposite of the three orientations Jay embodied. If we are caught up in our thoughts and what others think of us, we will be insecure. If we are clinging to static, declarative identities (I am a failure, I'm not good, I will never), we will remain locked in the prison such certitudes create. If we believe we are separate and isolated, we will be unable to find the creative trust and flow of collaboration and co-creation.

These modern categories are hard to shake and shift out of when they are still so predominant.

Postmodernism critiqued these grand narratives of modernism but, in its skepticism toward all objectivity, threw the baby out with the bathwater, and the bath, too, and maybe even the person bathing the baby, and the stool they sat on. Then they burned down the room and the house (you get the picture), leaving us fraught with an "everything is relative" and "everything is subjective" ambiguity.

And in the wake of such an outlook of cynical pessimism, the cyborg age was born. Technology could replace the metanarrative that once made us feel like we were a part of something together. Technology would create a perfect knowledge beyond subjectivity. Information, and more information, and faster information will define reality and save us from the inconvenience of being human.

But what has ultimate knowledge, or more information, given us? Has more information solved our economic inequity? Has Google obliterated racism? Has ChatGPT healed the ecological crisis? Has Meta healed your anxiety? Do the speed and convenience of algorithms replace your own hunger to fully express what is in your soul?

I'm not declaring that technologies are evil or pointless but rather that, while those tools are incredibly useful for many purposes, they are the wrong tools for helping us *feel more alive*. It's like trying to play a cello with a saw. Technology will only exacerbate the mind/body split. All social media "connection" ironically disconnects us further from our bodies, each other, and this planetary body.

In our obsession with expediting the process, we have forgotten that the process *is* the product. In treating bodily-ness as problematic, we have become disembodied, forgetting how to feel the pleasure, wonder, and joy in the slow, steady, sweat-filled making of art, life, love. In treating knowledge as synonymous with information, we have forgotten wisdom.

The erotic-creative worldview invites back the fleshy, unhurried, sensual seduction and orgasmic reclamation of the process. By seeing the process as the product, the challenge, work, and effort making requires is not seen as problematic any more than lovers would view the time, physicality, and exertion of lovemaking as problematic.

The time making takes is not an inconvenience.

When I am in the studio working on a song, I'm not wishing for a quicker, more convenient way to create. I am fully in my body, loving every second and anticipating what is coming, recognizing that what we are making is not just my own becoming but an offering for us all together. Art is the bastion for our humanity because it requires us to come back to ourselves, to be in our bodies, to *feel it all*, even as it points to an imaginal horizon of more.

Emerging eco-philosophers such as Andreas Weber and Bayo Akomolafe are radically shifting the focus into an orientation that feels far more aligned with an erotic-creative approach to life. Ecologically, they are exploring how the nature of our being is intradependent and related but with a crucial distinction: the body finally becomes the focus of that pursuit, understanding it as the only way wisdom is metabolized. The body's way of knowing is finally centered as a philosophy (as a way of loving wisdom) through touching, penetrating, feeling, sensing, animating, and softly surrendering . . . in every facet of this agony and ecstasy found in the limits and fragility of fleshiness.

The *erotic embodied experience* of love and longing is not secondary to reason but is the poetic thread that binds us together and to every other living thing in this life. According to Weber, the process is *enlivenment*, which is also the outcome of living with such sensual, attentive, unhurried presence.

At last, the weight of our bodily being has become a welcome seduction of gravity pinning us down, holding us here in its erotic embrace. It is nature who finally puts us on our backs, helping us forget every lofty abstraction we keep projecting upward and away from this earth. It is the bodily communing here and now that finally unravels and dissolves the projected distance between us and all that meta-glory—those perfected arrivals we became refugees of this earthy reality to get to.

Such sensual entanglement liberates us from modernity's inflated and insecure "I" to an enlivened, reciprocal "we." Such erotic enfleshment liberates us also from the cyborgian augmented reality and convenience and brings us back home to our own perfectly imperfect incarnation.

This shift is not a lofty philosophy; it is as intimate as your next breath. When I find myself feeling insecure or spiraling up and out of my body (often after having gotten lost in a scroll of a feed), I have a choice. If I continue to spiral in comparisons, worry, or self-doubt, my creativity is hostage, as are my joy and love. If, however, I put down my phone and come back to my body, allowing sensation to arouse my full awareness of the present moment, the spiraling stops. Then there's another step I take that fully brings me back to my own creative freedom: I *(re)member.* I don't mean this as in a nostalgic glance at the past, but rather I become membered to the "we" that "I" am once more. I expand my awareness outward to (re)member that "I" am not alone at all and because of that, I have everything I need. When you shift from the tired, modern concept of the separate-self "me" to the interconnected, ecological "we," your sense of support expands like the root systems of a tree. You can draw up a sense of connection, support, patience, and courage when you need it most, whether it's taking a creative risk, walking on stage, or having a difficult conversation.

So how do we shift from that separate, solo self to the erotic, entangled *we*?

Think about how everything living is a system of entangled relationships. There is no singular cell separate from the relational processes that sustain it. Our bodies, too, are a complex relationship of biological communities, your gut alone playing host to thousands of strains of bacteria that literally keep you alive. "You" couldn't "be" without the relationship with "them." Even our skin is porously mingling; the "boundaries" of our bodies are constantly being crossed in a fluid, viral exchange. There is also the relationship between you and the food you eat, which represents the complexity of relations not just directly to the animal or plant you put in your mouth but the systems that farmed, raised, harvested, packaged, shipped, or drove those goods to a farmer's stand or grocery store where you purchased it.

Beyond those relationships, there are the relationships you have with other humans and more-than-humans in your environment. Where you call home, the resources you use to stay alive, the living networks that metabolize your being . . . from the trees that transform carbon dioxide into oxygen you breathe to the waste workers who pick up your trash.

Then there's the way these relationships not only enliven you physically but emotionally and spiritually form part of what you could constitute as your communal lungs. The haunts you walk, the trees you pass daily, the rain that beads on your lashes and that you taste on your lips. Your friendships, your loved ones, and even the seemingly "random" matrix of relational exchanges you interact with daily on your commute, at work, at the park, on a trip.

You are a complex relational network that makes "you" possible, and your being (who you are) is ever becoming. We are never fixed, whole, complete. We are always in the flux of change (decay, growth, insights, relations, conceptions, imaginings).

We are Pieholden studio, the aging bricks and mortar *and* vulnerable human flesh, the building *and* its inhabitants. The tape is rolling, and everything is participating in the making of an album that is never finished, never done expressing. We are our relationships as we explore, deepen, and create. Our identities in this ontological view are not fixed/essential little Newtonian separate selves . . . they are flux-like, fluidly dynamic, unfinished, ever shifting, ever becoming. This ontological perspective takes the obsession with knowing, with having a map, and burns it in the pyre as it invites you *to experience* the journey of life on the path of no arrival.

This doesn't mean we don't hold individuation or that your perspective, feelings, experiences don't uniquely matter. Quite the opposite. In fact, you become more your "self" the more the "whole resounds" in your unique experience of it. This is something that mystical scholars like Cynthia Bourgeault affirm. Bourgeault teaches what defines your personhood, explaining a possible understanding of the etymology of *person* in the Latin (*per-sonare*) as one through whom the whole resounds. The freedom of shifting out of a fixed, self-enclosed identity is truly creative and empowering. Once you understand yourself as a system of relationships and always becoming, you'll no longer waste your energy trying to protect a fragile separate identity. You'll be liberated to actively participate in the making of new possibilities because your "me" will shift to a "we." And that freedom will make you curious, creative, playful.

I remember when I was a teenager, becoming serious about music, my friend Kent saying to me, "Don't do music because you want it to be an identity or a career. Do music because it makes you into a certain kind of person, someone who relates in a certain way to the world around you." What he said in a passing comment stuck like Velcro to my heart, the recognition that creativity is incompatible with a static identity. It would be like saying that taxidermy is an accurate description of a beast in the wild. Identities are shells of the living, not capable of holding the truth of what the living essence reveals in its dynamic unfolding freedom. When we cling to identities, or project them, we are clinging to an enclosure, a static costume that limits our lives in accordance with the limited room that costume provides. It's declaring that the product is finished rather than in process.

If I don't have to protect my identity anymore, if my identity isn't the insecure "I" that needs to be protected, then I'm freed to be about bigger, more reciprocally enlivening aims. The goal is not about an arrival, a destination, a merit, or proving my worth. It's about the process of (our) being as it continues to become. Instead of making declaratives to myself, saying incredibly negative or simply static identities ("I am a failure," "I'm no good"), I can shift into seeing myself as a gerund, as "learning," "expressing," "growing," "loving," "living." When that shift happens, there is no failure. There is no limiting story or belief. *The process is the product.*

My willingness to be here in the present with my whole body is to feel and experience myself as more-than-me, radically enough (satiety) *even while* I'm in process (openness to moreness, to a hunger beyond my satiety). By my embodied presence in the here and now, I am *also* welcoming of possibility in the may-yet-be. The more radically present I am here, in a confident, pleasurable, and playful way, the more possibility I can welcome. This is the source of my creative confidence.

This is the creative act. Which is love, which is creativity, which is life . . .

(Be) coming together.

No, this is not a formula. This isn't a linear progression or thesis. These three occurrences of shifting into embodied being, orienting toward the potential coming, and feeling how we are in this together play simultaneously like the three notes of a chord . . . they are harmonically co-resonant. They are the ingredients that make the process feel as good as the hoped-for outcome.

(be)Coming together is the unselfconscious, unapologetic, and pleasurably unhurried "here" and "arriving" stance of all lovers. It is the "present future tense" of all creatives, which Jay embodied so well.

To *Be* is to willingly choose to be erotically enthralled in the experience of embodied presence, to feel yourself at a sensory level in this moment. It is the practice of radical enough-ness we'll explore in more detail in the second half of this book. It is learning how to be fully *in* the experiential, embodied here and now . . . to be "turned on" in full present awareness in the body.

Coming is unlearning the distrust of what is coming, of the unknown, and shifting instead to an outlook of playful possibility (open to the unimagined potential of "yet"). It is learning how to befriend uncertainty instead of constantly fighting against it. It is to be seduced by the secret unknown future, oriented to the creativity of what could be . . . moment by moment.

Together is to recognize the self as only defined by the generous relational reciprocity that forms us. To see the gift of your life, love, creativity as an enlivening that enlivens—to see a gift that is made real by being given.

Like a lover who selflessly orients toward the beloved, the offering of your creativity to this world isn't a sacrifice or duty . . . it's the highest act of love in devotion. And it is pleasurable, purposeful, meaningful. Not because it's easy but because the friction and tension can be welcomed as part of the process of lovemaking, of art-making, of life-making. It doesn't mean there won't be deaths or heartbreak or hardships but that through it all, you choose the radical trust to believe that in every ending, there is a hidden new beginning . . . because this becoming together never really ends. It is never finished. There is always another song to sing, a line to write, a hue to paint . . . and that stance makes you humble, creative, *alive.*

And the tape rolls on.

And you let go of the safety of certitudes as you sing your heart out into the unknowing darkness.

The tiny flames of hope flicker like stars in the night, like candles in a warehouse studio . . . trembling at the sound of your voice, embracing your vulnerability with beauty, pleasure, and playfulness.

Which makes your vulnerability even more beautiful because you feel the intimacy of what you are offering in the unhurried enlivening you both experience and give.

And this is what art is/does. Because art imitates life in this radical generosity, in this abundant, thrilling reciprocity. Love is made in what we give away.

Our purpose and our meaning are wrapped up in that giving. Not for the sake of an arrival point. Not to shore up an identity. Not for an idea of perfection.

But for creativity's own sake because it feels good to make, and love, and live this way.

I can still hear Jay's voice as it echoes down the elevator shaft:

Because, darling . . . the process is the product.

Chapter Five

~~Good~~ Great Lovers
The Generosity of Generativity

> *All art is a gift. It is first of all a gift that the maker can do it. It is then a gift to someone else, whether they pay for it or not. . . . Art is life seeking itself.*
>
> —Vincent Van Gogh

"I don't even know where to begin."

"AT THE BEGINNING, YOU MORON," Kat yelled through the other end of the line. I laughed at her impatience. I was sitting in one of my vintage silk kimonos staring at the way the late-morning sun was streaming through my window and lighting up the leaves of my banana leaf plant, sipping my second cup of coffee as I talked on the phone with one of my dearest friends.

"Okay, okay, okay." I grinned. "Well, get comfortable."

The Wanderer—let's call him W—and I met on a dating app. Yes, the cliché not-meet-cute of every millennial and younger. The pandemic, while still very much running our lives, was on its second wave, and those of us who had survived the madness single came bursting out of our houses in what has now been described as the postpandemic summer of love.

Basically, I had not been touched by any adult human in almost two years. Yes, I had my kids, but that was different. It got so bad that on several nights after getting the kids to bed, I scrunched myself against the stairway wall to feel like the walls were holding me. And on one very notable occasion, I walked into Dick's sporting goods (yes, that is an actual store) masked to get the kids some sports balls, and I walked right up to a male mannequin and hugged it. I just couldn't remember what "man-body" felt like. Granted, this guy's abs were rock hard, but so was the rest of his body. Didn't really satisfy the itch, even if it entertained onlookers.

When it seemed like socialization was back on the table, I was READY TO DATE again. I hopped on the apps friends recommended, quickly becoming disillusioned with both the experience and the options. As I was living in West Michigan, the feed of guys who came up were essentially "dude with a fish," "dude with a fish," "dude with a hunting rifle," "dude at sports event," "dude with a fish." Here and there I had a couple of dates, mostly woefully uninspired. This is why when W came up, a dreamboat, photographer New Yorker with an all-out artist vibe who was coming through town, I swiped right.

"Wait. First, what did you end up wearing?" Kat asked.

"I settled for jean shorts, a white tank top, and one of my kimonos. You know, the whole 'I'm not trying, but I look better than if someone else was trying.'"

She laughed. "Yup, very you. So tell me everything. I'm dying!"

"Okay. Sorry, my . . . uh . . . mind and body are a little short-circuited at the moment." I cleared my throat. "Okay . . . so it all started when I watched him pull up and get out of the car."

W was tall—six feet, three inches maybe—but he moved fluidly and unhurried in a way that was almost feline in its grace. He looked like a taller, tanner, and slightly sexier Jeff Buckley. His face lit up when he saw me, and the combination of that devastating smile, those lips and those brown eyes, and his quiet, rumbled "hey" ruined something in me forever. We hugged, and it was like some ancient olfactory evolutionary recognition cued my body that this was a decent basketful of chromosomal successful genetic mating material. Even in the hug, it all felt too "thank you, yes," "oh . . . fuck," and "wow." Which explains perhaps why when I went to sit down on the outdoor settee, I missed it by about a foot.

"OH MY GOD." Kat laughed so hard on the phone it literally took her five minutes to stop crying and snorting.

Yeah. Super sexy of me to fall on my ass. Reaaaallllly smooth. *Ultimate* cool.

"Holy shit, are you okay?" He quickly helped me back to my traitorous feet.

"Clearly no, not at all." I laughed. We stood there for a minute, still hanging on to each other, laughing. Our eyes locked, and time suspended. Was I breathing? *Breathe, Brie!* I could feel my cheeks burning. Hell, all of me was burning.

He tilted his head to the side and looked at me then with an expression I would come to love. It was a quizzical kind of wonder . . . a half smile and a slight squint that looked like a question, amazement, and delight rolled into one. He seemed deeply amused by the combination of my unbridled laughter at myself, the very clear impact he was having on me in that eternal moment of staring at each other, and the way my mind was whirring at a speed that not only made talking difficult but apparently impaired my basic motor function as well.

And thus began my first night with W. We talked for hours, late into the night. We moved from sitting on the patio to the living room, where he sat on the sofa and I sat across the coffee table on the ground (where gravity couldn't betray me further). I noticed the way he moved and the way he sat. He was utterly in his body and totally in the present—at ease in a way that wasn't domineering like I had experienced so often with guys, the way they project their charisma or persona out loudly to hide insecurities. W was totally in himself, and in the moment, and not at all intimidated by me . . . by my mind or creativity, by my being a single mom, or any other aspect of my "much-ness."

Because he was also an artist, he noticed things about me, my house, my paintings in a way that made me feel seen . . . seen beyond the mind, beyond ideas. Appreciated in a way that was present to who I dynamically was.

What radiated out of W's confidence through his embodied being was nothing short of mesmerizing. The curve of his arm behind his head, the way his other hand rested by his side. And eventually as the distance between us lessened, the way his hand reached out to gently brush my hair out of my face. There were words I was saying. I stopped knowing what they were. Word soup was coming out of my mouth. So many words. Word-y word, words. I was still talking when his hand cupped my cheek, his thumb slowly trailing down my jawline to my mouth (why the hell was I still talking?). His thumb brushed across my lower lip as he spoke.

"I love listening to you. I think I could listen to you forever." His eyes went from mine to where his thumb still rested. And then his mouth was on mine. Pulling back just for a moment to murmur, "I'm still listening" against my lips. But I wasn't talking anymore.

What followed was an experience that made my body feel the physical equivalent of going from staring at a pixelated videotape from the '90s to 8k UHD. It's not that I hadn't had great sex before, I'm way too passionate of a person to not express that passion in all the ways. But this . . . this was totally *other.* It was the most tender, unhurried, generous, luscious, pleasure-filled, and loving reciprocity . . . a modality of being and becoming, of communication and movement, of absolute unselfconscious freedom and total permission that we lavished generously on each other.

And as I consider what it was that made my experience with W that night, and many other subsequent nights, stand out, it was his radical embodied presence, the way he was so unhurried, so not in his head, so *with me* . . . like he had nothing to prove and nowhere to get to. Hours upon hours of touching, being touched, breathing, gasping, feeling . . . then laughing and talking in between.

At some point, I fell asleep. And for the first time, I didn't wake up in the middle of the night with cold sweat and a racing heart, in confused panic at the sound of a man sleeping beside me. I woke up in the middle of the night, totally at ease in myself . . . content. W's golden, tan arm was draped over my hip, my back against his chest. *Wait, what?* I *never* cuddled like this long enough to fall asleep entangled. I trailed my finger down his arm. *Why is his skin so soft? Does the water in Brooklyn have, like, microscopic fairies that buff his skin to make it this soft?* I curled my body further against his, and even in sleep, he wrapped his arm tighter around my body, burrowing his face into me and kissing the back of my head. I fell back to sleep and woke up to our hands clasped together.

Over the course of our two-year unhurried love affair of occasional encounters, W helped lots of things rewire and heal. Not just the residuals of the assault, but he helped me shed earlier stories too. Most of my inherited beliefs about sexuality and bullshit purity culture had long been burned at the pyre of my becoming, but while my mind had moved on, the somatic impact of those stories was harder to get to. What we shared as lovers was generous. It was free and freeing. It was enlivening enlivenment. It was *gift*.

It was . . . *thank you, yes. Also . . . fuck. And wow.*

Falling into abundance feels like that. Like it's almost too good to be true. Which is why our brains short-circuit a little when we're gifted these kinds of experiences of *more*. Most of us have been well trained to suppress the possibility of more, to corset our imaginations into a more moderate shape and expect what is *reasonable* to expect. Avoid disappointment. Better to keep those expectations low. Just *assume* that the pixelated videotape life is as good as it gets.

That response makes sense when we consider maybe we're all still grieving the loss of magic in our lives. We're given wonderment and enchantment through Santa Claus or the Tooth Fairy, only to be told later it's a lie. We're told to reach for the stars and dream big when you are young, only to be told in college you have to pick a major out of the premade list of available options that can provide a steady, reliable income. We're fed magical stories of trees that talk, forests full of woodland fairies, and portals to other worlds hidden inside our world, only to be taught in school that we humans are the only real sentient beings here, and matter can't feel.

All that magic? Yeah, it's not really real. Grow up. Expect less. Want less.

Bereft of that anything-is-possible sparkle of joyful expectation in our eyes, we've lost the ability to see the miraculous hidden in plain sight. So sometimes it takes an experience of gift—of a total body, heart, and mind short-circuiting—to help you rewire the way you look at life. Sometimes it takes a surge of *moreness* to begin seeing the more in everything. Sometimes it takes a moment of pure magic to remember the magic all around you.

But having a short-circuiting kind of magical experience isn't the only way to shift from "sensible" scarcity to believing in the wild wondrous (although thank the gods for those experiences). That mind-blowing shift is a switch we have access to. We flip the switch when we choose to be turned on to the erotic currents all around us, the life-force moving miraculously in the midst of what we've declared menial. We flip the switch when we choose to open our senses to the sensational.

When I was seventeen, a friend of mine introduced me to the poetry of Pablo Neruda. I didn't know much about poetry then, besides the cursory high-school exposure to it. But when

I read that worn copy of Neruda's poems, it felt like a switch had been turned on in me, and suddenly the world was filled with diaphanous luminosity. His "Odes to Common Things" transformed the most average utensil or vessel into a thing of startling splendor, wonder, and love. The more I read, the more I began to see the world as brimming with beauty, his erotic superfluity filling my body and soul to overflowing. Suddenly every object was worth praising, every moment worth pausing, *every thing* worth naming as precious, sacred, and irreplaceable.

The poets teach us to see the world through the gaze of love, of wonder, of astonishment. They teach us to appreciate what is hidden in plain sight. They gift us the sight we almost lost. They bring back magic.

Seeing through the eyes of the poets is a way of shifting back into believing in the *moreness* once more. Through their devotion to attention, they show us the way back to wonderment. And the more we pay attention, the more we begin to appreciate how miraculous this life really is. The more we recognize it as *gift*.

Inspiration does that. The word *inspire* means to encourage and animate, but it also literally means to breathe in. And in this case, when we see life as *gift*, we are breathing in that kind of magical reverence. As all singers know, the quality of your inhale is what determines your exhale. So what we are breathing in—what we are choosing to see and believe about the world around us—is metabolized in us as what we give. As the famous spiritual maxim says, energy floes where attention goes. The world is as wondrous as our ability to perceive it as such, or, as Rilke exclaimed in "Letters to a Young Poet," "If your daily life seems to lack material, do not blame it; blame yourself, tell yourself that you are not poet enough to summon up its riches; for there is no lack for him who creates and no poor, trivial place."

This erotic wonderment is not just a "see the glass half full" kind of gratitude I'm speaking of here. It is a "*thank you . . . yes.*

Also, fuck. And wow" approach to loving, relating, creating that doesn't just shift how *you see* but how you *live*. When you're not coming at life from a mindset of scarcity, abundance frees you to become a wildly generous lover and a generative maker. The more you perceive life as gift, the more you'll *want* to give this life everything you are. The more you'll want to give yourself away wildly, extravagantly, abundantly.

When creative desire (which is what I consider life, love, and art to be) is motivated by this holy-wow generosity, it moves beyond you into the *more-than-you*. It is a love-fueled longing that has nothing to do with having, getting, or controlling. Rather, it seeks to give itself away, to animate *moreness* in those you gift yourself to and beyond.

In *The Gift: How the Creative Spirit Transforms the World*, Lewis Hyde offers his basic premise: "If the object is a gift, it keeps moving." Approaching life from this unselfish largess is a loaves-and-fishes, more-leads-to-more multiplication of the "power of yes" kind of math. It is a posture of making in which the *process is the product* and the gift is in the giving. Which means the more generous you are with your loving, living, making, the more generative your loving, living, making become:

> Gift exchange and erotic life are connected in this regard. The gift is an emanation of Eros, and therefore to speak of gifts that survive their use is to describe a natural fact: libido is not lost when it is given away. Eros never wastes his lovers. When we give ourselves in the spirit of that god, he does not leave off his attentions; it is only when we fall to calculation that he remains hidden and no body will satisfy. Satisfaction derives not merely from being filled but from being filled with a current that will not cease. With the gift, as in love, our satisfaction sets us at ease because we know that somehow its use at once assures its plenty.

It's interesting that when we experience a piece of great art, we exclaim, "I'm so touched" or "That really moved me." We intuit that what is happening in those moments of awe and wonder is that we are being transformed, rewired, and that our world has been shifted somehow. The switch gets flipped, and we are filled with a buoyant sense of that magical *moreness* . . . and yeah, it short-circuits us a little. Our bodies feel momentarily weightless or speared through by ecstatic beauty, and such beauty blows our minds. Which makes sense because our minds are the domain of assessing, predicting, anticipating, and measuring. The mind perceives through differentiation, comparison, and is oriented toward security. It's constantly scanning for possible threats. That's what the mind should be doing . . . and what has evolutionarily assured our survival. What happens when Eros voltage comes in is that we (re)member—we become membered to—more of ourselves than just our minds. Our bodies and hearts come back online, and we feel our way into a soulful expansion that reconnects us not just to ourselves but to each other . . . a shift that invites a softening of our fear that yields a trust in a greater possibility, a willingness to believe in *more.*

And this is the gift of Love (Eros, Art, Inspiration). . . it moves us from scarcity to abundance. From fear to a creative trust.

One of my favorite philosophers and theologians, Beatrice Bruteau, describes this shift as a movement from a "domination paradigm" into a creative "communion paradigm." Domination, that fear-based response to the unknown we've explored in this book (and a central instinct of Eurocentric humanity), is so familiar, it's almost a default. When faced with any vast, untraveled, wild territory, culture, or noncategorized reality, the instinct to colonize or conquer, subjugate, and deplete resources reigns supreme. It reinforces established dualities, continuously splitting the field of experiential embodied reality into body/spirit, inside/outside, living beings/nonliving matter. Bruteau defines it this way: "Domination is an asymmetrical, or nonreciprocal, relation of determination of being: of what the being is, or of what it is, or of how it can act, or of how it is to be valued." The domination paradigm pits the self against the other, human against nature, and views the cosmos through a lens of scarcity, and therefore competition and comparison.

You might be thinking, "Oh yeah, that's evil, systemic stuff," but scratch the surface of daily life, and you'll locate the same domination paradigm in the air we breathe, in what we imbibe and spew out ourselves. Its influence is felt in how we even think of ourselves psychologically, spiritually, and otherwise. The domination paradigm functions as a pyramid of *power-over*, to use a term coined by ecologist Joanna Macy. And if you look carefully, you can see traces of this power-over pyramid (where the objective or goal is "us" against "them," climb to "get to the top," and have more power/success/money than those on the bottom) just about everywhere in culture.

Everything in life is *quantitatively* measured by this economy of domination: financial success as determining personal success. Meaning as only found in having, in winning, in mastery of the game, and from an external validation of approval, fame, and recognition. Anything perceived as failure is a "death" to be avoided at all costs.

In contrast to this all-too-familiar worldview is the communion paradigm. Bruteau describes it as a "symmetrical, reciprocal relation of enhancement of being: that beings may be, may become all that they can be, may act in maximum freedom and be valued for their incomparable preciousness. Here I am I by virtue of being in-you/with-you/for-you, not outside and not against-not even separate."

Instead of the dominion of *power-over*, this alternative paradigm is a reciprocal *power-with*. Instead of a pyramid of competition, it places us in a web of *connection*, in a rhizomatic fungal network intertwined with roots. It's an earthen, biological way of understanding ourselves as inherently connected. Within that transition from starkly outlined borders to intertwining of roots, our motivation and desire shift from being hijacked by insecure personal aims to a *radial* enlivening (an enlivening that enlivens others radially around you). It moves you into generosity, into gift.

This is not a utopian ideal. What Bruteau describes for us is a shift from fearful control to creative trust. Instead of separation, threat, and competition, we choose instead to live from a secure sense of shared belonging, from an appreciating plenitude and desire for the abundance of co-creativity. "The drive to create," says Bruteau, "comes forward as more fundamental and yields a deeper satisfaction than the desire for gain or protection."

Creativity (Eros, love, life) thrives in environments of power-with. Likewise, creativity (Eros, love, life) will shrivel and die in environments of power-over.

If you are a musician, you know and have experienced the communion paradigm when you step into the studio with your band; a womblike energy becomes tangible in which you feel like you're "in this thing" together. . . . like you're a part of a secret, and you are. You are cocreating and birthing art through reciprocity, trust, and collaboration. Or perhaps if you've acted, you can recall the feeling that comes over the cast of a play as you approach curtains up, the way you move in a coordinated choreography with the cast and crew and feed off each other's momentum. Or maybe you can think of a specific project at work when your team flowed in that reciprocal, creative trust. Or maybe you can recall a time you were in the kitchen cooking with friends (the kind of friends you don't have to explain things to or task with jobs), and you seemed to dance around each other with such joy and ease that you could swear the meal was *that* much tastier for it.

I'm sure you can just as easily think of situations like the above when one person (maybe it was you) suddenly spiraled into insecurity, doubt, or mistrust of your team, friends, or colleagues. What happened next? Perhaps it felt like the oxygen left the room. Things got tense and awkward. The creativity floundered or maybe was wholly put out.

When Desire (Eros) is filtered through fear, it results in our trying to *control life*. When you see yourself as an isolated, separate self, as "me against the world," it's likely you will hedge in and cling to certitudes to shore up your sense of safety and security. You will be competitive and obsessed with arrivals and achievements driven by an imagined need to prove your worth. "Never enough!" will become your mantra. Your life will become about *having* more, not *being or gifting more*. This is the goal of domination: power-over circumstances . . . relationships . . . resources, by propagating the lie that you are what you *possess or prove*.

In contrast, Desire (Eros) filtered through a communal trust results in an effort to *give more life*. Gifting our creative energy for the sake of experiencing and sharing enlivenment with others. Instead of being driven by "never enough," you will see yourself as more-than-enough. You will be grounded in a sense of satisfaction *and* creativity because that is what love engenders. Your life will be defined by what you generate, by how alive you are, and how you can serve and inspire others.

Enlivenment, pleasure, and possibility are all given the more we recognize the gift of our shared becoming, loving, creating. The gift-giver is paradoxically given a gift in the giving. And the gift grows radially and keeps on giving, which is the nature of the dynamism of erotic generosity Lewis Hyde describes. This was also the gift I experienced with W, where the aim of our lovemaking was not a selfish possession, "getting off" or "having." It was an unhurried, presently embodied, utterly comfortable in "being" tender, vulnerable in an unfolding "becoming" reciprocation of enlivenment. It was a generous "I am" that simultaneously engendered an ecstatic "may you be."

In life, creativity, or in the best of spirituality, there's this same harmonizing key change. When you move from the dissonance of a life that is just about you to the harmonic fullness of allowing your life to flow into *more-than-you*, which is the creative act, *more life flows in and out of you.*

An erotic-creative relational guideline could perhaps then be found in this fundamental choice in the aim of our desire: the choice to control life or to gift life through our creativity. To constantly be asking in all categories of our lives, "Am I trying to control or create?" "Am I trying to possess or *gift?*" To examine our decisions against the choice to hem life in or to let life out. The choice between being selfish/egoic or creative/communal.

Life is hemmed in and limited by a worldview of scarcity, but it is erotically enlivened by a worldview of abundance. Said another way, cowardice controls; courageousness creates.

For me, the distinction between domination (control) and communion (creativity) provides helpful tools for discerning how I'm channeling my Eros, my life-force, my creativity. Am I responding to this circumstance, person, relationship from control, out of fear? Can I shift into a communing trust that cocreates? Can I shift into offering my love, creativity, life as . . . *gift*?

Good lovers are great not because they perform Olympic-level sex moves (although Lord knows many men still think that's the ticket) or because they successfully bring you to orgasm. Good lovers are great because of their generosity and embodied presence. The way their grounded, unhurried, and nonanxious being relaxes and creates space for your grounded, relaxed, embodied being. Good lovers are great because of their capacity to flow with you into greater and greater depths of (unknowing) intimacy and tenderly stay there in that vulnerability *with you*. Good lovers are great because their capacity to relate to you deepens, and in the deepened relating, they don't claim any knowledge of you as something fixed they can possess but rather reverence you for who you are as an unfolding mystery, a dynamic becoming forever beyond their grasp . . . *and love you for it.*

Good lovers are *great* because they make your pleasure their own and so move ecstatically beyond their desire into a greater desire. Great lovers are about the gift.

I don't just want to be a good lover of life . . . I want to be a *great* lover of this life. Someone whose life is marked by a willingness to give everything that I am away in every song, every word, every touch, every embrace. When we comment on someone's creative capacity, we sometimes exclaim, "They are so *gifted.*" Perhaps we are intuitively connecting the creative as being determined by one's capacity to generously offer their gift to the world with abandon. Sure, you can be a good artist and still be an asshole and make everything all about you. The entertainment industries have tried to make art about money and possession, and their platforms are rife with examples of self-obsession and fragile narcissism. But if you hunger (as I do) not for the prescribed "good" life of *having more* but the great life, a life that is greater than you and oriented toward *making more*—your desire, Eros (creativity, love, life), will only increase as you learn to ecstatically make it about more-than-you.

In each moment, I hope my exhales sound like ecstatic sighs of gratitude. I want my body to be present to every moment like the arousal enlivenment between lovers and with an orgasmic *yes*. Even when things are hard, which they often are, I want to be the kind of person who utters this prayer of poetic appreciation in each moment and with the whole of her life:

Thank you, yes. Also, fuck. And . . . wow.

Like a lover whose mind and body have been short-circuited by love.

* * *

When we live from such plenitude, it is natural to be enraptured by this world and this life . . . delighted and in awe and amused all at once. You *want* to be about creating more life, not controlling it. About gifting yourself and your creativity, not having or possessing. Like a great lover, you will be oriented toward giving because your desire becomes and grows as it moves toward more-than-you.

If the movement of life can be trusted on its way to more life, then the movements of your life into greater possibility can be trusted too. But it is one thing to understand this erotic approach to life with your mind and another thing to begin to live it in your body in the midst of your everyday life. It's one thing to talk about love; it's another thing to be in the throes of making it. It's one thing to see an instrument and a whole different thing to learn how to play it.

So . . . let's play, shall we?

Act II

Turning Yourself On

Erotic Applications for the Creative Life

The Climax

Climax *(cli-max): (1) a figure of speech in which a series of phrases or sentences is arranged in ascending order of rhetorical forcefulness. (2) the point of highest dramatic tension or a major turning point in the action (as of a play). (3) orgasm.*

—Oxford Languages

Maybe such devotion, in which one holds the world
In the clasp of attention, isn't the perfect prayer,
But it must be close, for the sorrow, whose name is doubt,
Is thus subdued, and not through the weaponry of reason,
But of pure submission. Tell me, what else
Could beauty be for?[1]

—Mary Oliver

Let's say you and I have been dating for a while now . . . months, maybe even a year. Where in the beginning of this book (in the early days), my stories were shared in the first blush of love, now we know each other well . . . our movements, voices, and mannerisms all far more familiar. We have fallen in love. And as you know from your own experiences with that great plummet into great love, familiarity does not exhaust the mystery of the other before you. There are always more stories to share, more details to learn, more discoveries that surprise, astonish, and delight one another. Love makes us forget the poverty of who we thought we were before and helps us (re)member (become membered to) a moreness we could have never imagined.

So while perhaps stories were once shared shyly, like Polaroids and Post-it notes, now they reveal themselves between the tangle of sheets with the ease of intimacy, in unhurried morning conversations over coffee, and in the natural, practical realities of running errands or cooking a meal together.

The disclosure of a beloved's memories is both a discovery of their unique experiences and, in that knowledge, a bond that you share, a deepening of your love. And Love becomes a (re)membering in this way: each memory your lover shares invites your own memories to likewise be offered to the growing love between you. Each story they disclose elicits your own to be revealed. Intimacy creates the art of reciprocal vulnerability. And because Love unravels the defenses, the walls of fear around our hearts, I cannot help but share more stories with you now . . . to let you see more of me, to let you in more fully. To give you more of myself that you might know me and, in that knowing, remember and know *yourself* more fully. That together we might (re)member ourselves in love.

* * *

"AGAIN?" His tiny hands were cupped together and outstretched high above him like a little devoted disciple taking communion. His eyes were sparkling, his face shining with joy. He giggled and splashed his chubby legs impatiently. "AGAIN? AGAIN, MAMA???"

Smiling, I scooped a huge amount of water in the giant cup and held it high above him and slowly tipped the cup until a small perfect trickle of water came down into his little hands below. The diamond droplets sparkled as they bounced off him and all over his face, clinging to his wet hair and eyelashes in little crystal beads. His shrieks of laughter filled the bathroom, a sound so dynamic it made the bathroom of the old house we lived in reverberate like a great hall, and my heart wouldn't have known the difference between this tub and the Grand Ole Opry.

"AGAIN?" he looked up at me grinning, full of expectation. Of course, I indulged.

How many times had I poured out the water? How long had I been sitting there? Was the water even warm anymore? None of that mattered.

For a parent, these moments are the eternal ones . . . the ones that live on in my heart, feed me joy . . . beauty . . . gratitude and will do so till my dying day. They are so not because they were imbued with any more wonder or magic than any other. No. They are eternal simply because I was fully present in them . . . present with my whole body, heart, and mind and surrendered to the magic of being in the thrall of wonder with my children.

"What is *really* most important?" these moments ask. Our hearts know the answer. Everything else falls away.

* * *

We huddled together on the side of the stage, the tulle of our skirts pressing against each other. The muffled clack of the toe shoes could be heard as a couple of dancers rushed to join the line. I was the tiniest dancer . . . over three years younger than the rest of my class. To accommodate my size, I was always featured in the center of the lineup. A stubborn, tiny thing, determined to be as good as the girls above me, I had earned the nickname Pitu (Smurf) due to my stature and the blue leotard I wore to class almost every day. The lights dimmed, and the curtain began to draw back . . . a hush fell over the audience. The music began. My count approaching, I stepped into the light. All the hard work, all the pain, sweat, and tears . . . all the stories of being too small, too short, too little. I wasn't thinking about any of those things. I gave my whole heart away in every movement.

"What defines perfection?" these moments ask.

Our hearts know the answer. Everything else falls away.

* * *

Tears stung in my eyes as I felt frustration and self-defeat. Trying all morning to work on the still life before me, all I had managed was multiple crumpled sheets of paper at my feet. I glanced over to my brother's impressive painting to my right. Great. Just great.

Everyone else around me was busy painting, the hiss of their paintbrushes on paper punctuated annoyingly by their easeful conversations. Meanwhile, I was still gripping the nub of charcoal and trying hard to contain the scream building in my throat.

Ramiro had already walked by me a few times, and it only made me feel more defeated that he shuffled on without saying anything, seemingly content to let me stew in my mounting nuclear combustion. I ripped the current disaster off the board and mounted another sheet, trying not to notice how the other kids beside me got quiet in what was obviously recriminating distaste at my incompetent wastefulness. The tears burned hotter and finally began falling.

"¿Qué tal, Gabi?" came Ramiro's soft voice. I turned. I probably could have guessed that my tear-streaked face was now also marked with charcoal. He came beside me and put his hand on my shoulder. "You are very passionate, and passion is good. But you have to learn how to wield it, or it will master you."

"My lines are all wrong. And everyone else has no problem," I whined.

"Ah, well, in order to draw lines, you have to breathe. Have you thought of breathing?" His eyes twinkled kindly as he took my charcoal. "The charcoal is an extension of your hand, of your arm . . . of your breath. We do not draw from the mind but from the body . . . observe. Breathe in . . . and . . ." He drew a continuous graceful line of form on his out breath. Then he handed the charcoal back to me and put his hand back on my shoulder. "You are fighting with yourself. Relax . . . breathe. You are overthinking, and you must trust the flow of movement. Your body knows what to do." He made it look so easy, so effortless . . . this trust of movement.

"Gracias, Ramiro," I grumbled out.

"Oh, and Gabi," he said quietly without looking back as he shuffled slowly away, "stop comparing yourself to your brother. Trust yourself."

"What determines an authentic expression of art?" these moments ask. Our hearts know the answer. Everything else falls away.

* * *

"I'm ninety percent certain this is illegal." I giggled into his neck. We were in a public park and definitely getting naked . . . specifically: getting naked in the river.

"Whatever. This is our primal animal right." He laughed as he unhooked my bra and tossed it onto the bank and returned to the business at hand. "Besides," he murmured between kisses and lifting me up till my legs wrapped around his waist, "we're literally in the middle of nowhere and haven't seen anyone all day."

The Maverick and I, let's call him M, had been out hiking all morning. The water was mountain cold and frankly freezing, but the sun was shining down on our wet (much more exposed) skin as we clung to each other . . . feeding ourselves with the warmth of our desire. The simultaneity of hot and cold was seductively enthralling, the rush of the river loud all around us lulling us into a world of our own making, which is how I later justified the fact that we did not at all hear the group of men approaching. One minute I was in the throes of what felt like a *Legends of the Fall*–level sex scene, and the next thing I knew I heard male voices. Close male voices. As in very close.

"Shit!" M cried out, unceremoniously tossing me back into the water as I crouched my body down into the river, which unfortunately only came up to my very exposed breasts, which I quickly covered with my arms in the nick of time before three very manly men rounded the bend and hiked by us on shore.

"Hey, guys," M said casually as he tried to shield me from view.

"Hey," said one amused dude looking over at us, "how's the . . . uh . . . water?"

"Oh, we're just taking a bath," I blurted out. *A bath?* "A bathing bath. A bath for bathing . . . for hygiene bodily cleansing purposes." I tried to ignore M's staring at me, willing me to stop the word-train-wreck coming out of my mouth. Jesus Christ, *way to play it cool, Stoner.* The other guys nodded as they continued on like they believed me *not at all.*

"Sounds, uh . . . refreshing," said the second guy. "But, uh . . . you may want to find a spot . . . I don't know, *off* the main trail." The first guy snorted as he stifled a laugh, while I turned in slow motion and stared open-mouthed at M.

"We're on the main trail???" I hissed to him in a whisper.

"Have a nice . . . bathing bath!" the last guy called out, not even trying to keep in his mirth. All of two seconds passed before we heard their unbridled laughter coming back to us from upriver.

"What the HELL, M???" I yelled while splashing him.

"What?" He laughed sheepishly. "We haven't seen anyone all day, have we? Now, uh . . . where were we with that *bathing* bath?" We both burst into laughter, and he swept me up again, and while I did keep one eye trained on the bend for any other hikers, we got back to our definitely not-bathing.

"Who gives a shit about what other people think?" these moments ask.

Our hearts know the answer. Everything else falls away.

"What is success?" these moments ask.

Our hearts know the answer. Everything else falls away.

What is courage? What is greatness? What does it feel like to be fully alive?

Our hearts know the answer. Everything else falls away.

Chapter Six

Turned On
Arousing Sensation for Embodied Presence

> ***Presence is far more intricate and rewarding an art than productivity.***
>
> —Maria Popova

His little body scrambled up to the piano stool, and he turned to where I had *just* sat down on the sofa and yelled, "Mama . . . let's pway PIANO!"

I was eight months pregnant with Ro and desperately trying to keep up with my three-year-old firstborn, Søren. I was So. Damn. Tired. Those days were endless eternities of sleep-deprived insanity, of Legos and finger food and Daniel Tiger, and "Mama, again?" I kicked toys on the floor out of the way to sit my pregnant ass next to him. To be a parent is to step willingly into madness. To be a pair of udders and 24/7 need-fulfillment center. And yet, and *yet* . . .

Like a diaphanous dimension that is glimpsed behind the veil of this one, another world arrives amid the clutter and in between the moments of exhaustion and chaos, a landscape of more love, more joy, just more. I swear I didn't know life could be so beautiful. The madness is worth it.

We sat down, and I let him play. His face lit up at the creative power, of being able to create such resonance. "Make a song, Mama?" I smiled. This was a thing we did. I would play a chord progression and sing, and he would add to it, playing along with me.

I was thirty years old. When I was younger, I thought I'd have several records out and have toured the world by thirty. I thought I'd be . . . *someone.* But as I began a little playful progression, I had this sense come over me like the warmth of a sunrise, a dawning knowing that had been growing in me: this moment (or any moment with Søren), and this song, was the kind of eternal magic that outshone any achievement or recognition in the world.

Even as tired as I was, I knew. As swollen and stretched out as my body was, I felt it. So I let my hands play, and my voice joined in as I made up a song for him.

Where could Søren be, where could Søren be? I don't know. I don't know.
We were playing hide and seek,
We were playing hide and seek . . .
Where did he go? Where did he go?

And as I played, his little smile beaming, his hands reverently and joyfully picked notes along the ivory keys to join in and add to our song.

I laughed because he was laughing. And I laughed because he was so rhythmic and his natural sense for melody was already surprising. And I laughed because underneath the exhaustion, there was always a wellspring of love keeping me afloat.

And I laughed because this life wasn't what I thought it would be.

It was *so much more.*

I didn't yet know that my life would one day hold both motherhood *and* a life of being a full-time musician, artist, and writer. But by my devotion to the present moment, the sweet yielding of my embodied yes was the climactic, pleasurable conception of that expansive dream.

The call of the artist is the call on every one of our human hearts to be fully present, *to really be here* so that we can be enthralled by the wonder all around us and, in our attention, to be swept into the current of beauty. To be fully present to the miracle of the magic that is coursing through our veins in each breath so we can actually feel and participate in weaving the unseen threads of love binding us to each other and to this world and to the stars.

The call of the artist (a title to which every human can lay claim) is to live a life in full, present attention to Love that keeps pouring out like a trickle of water delighting a toddler. Courage like a tiny dancer being willing to stand out. Generosity like that of the old master painter giving permission to his tiny students to believe themselves capable. Rebellious passion like two lovers who don't care about what other people think. Devotion to beauty that recognizes that the true accomplishments on this earth are what we make and give away, no matter how unseen the gift or the giving may seem.

The arousal of presence is the portal to all that is possible in this life. To the one horizon of human exploration that is above all others: the one that lays on the other side of everything we haven't yet imagined. And when we are not *here*, we miss it.

Embodied presence is being awake to the gift of this life in a somatic way that enlivens you. It's turning yourself on, allowing the body to heighten its sensory awareness, allowing you to relax and drop out of your mind and into the "enough-ness" of this moment and of yourself.

No transformation, insight, discovery, or creativity happens apart from the body. But weirdly, we more than often ambulate through our days like a walking mind that only occasionally remembers the body when it's hungry, thirsty, tired, or pushed during a workout. We treat our bodies with about the same amount of care as a terrible pet owner: "Oh, you're still here? With your needs and whatnot? How annoying."

The mind's perception functions through comparison and analysis. It only knows how to divide and conquer and creates binaries and narratives that *make sense* and are *reasonable.* So even as you sit and try to do nothing, your mind will likely tell you how you feel about sitting, will remind you that you have a lot more than nothing to do, and then will even judge how you're doing with the thinking-of-nothing task.

And the thing is, that's just what the mind does! It's not doing anything wrong. It's just that, like a computer, its program runs in ones and zeros, in comparison and contrast, in "this is right and that's wrong," which means the mind creates stories in which you're either succeeding or failing, getting things right or getting them wrong, a winner or a loser. In short, the mind comfortably employs the binary categories of the domination paradigm, the way of perception that only perceives in categorical dualities, because that's how our thinking kind of works.

Consider the stories that flare up during a conflict. Do you unconsciously create a good guy (probably you) and a bad guy (probably them)? Or think about what you're unconsciously doing when you're scrolling your feed . . . is some part of you comparing yourself? The mind does not do thought-free "presence." It analyzes presence and informs you if the pinpointed occurrence was good or bad. We cannot be present with the mind.

Only through the body can we be present. Only through sensation can we drop into a greater more-than-the-mind awareness. Only by turning the body on can the mind relax its faculties and let a different form of perception run the show. Instead of mind over matter, it's letting *more matter* than the mind's interpretation.

The path of the erotic creator is to drop into more-than-mind perception and create from that spaciousness. It's a lower center of gravity in which sensation helps to ground our awareness in the body, allowing us the freedom to make without collapsing into critique, judgment, or self-consciousness (although those feelings often rise up again after the fact like a vulnerability hangover).

It's the same place you drop into during sex when you're not in your head (we've all been there) but rather fully enraptured in the sensory presence of here and now with your lover.

Paradoxically, only in being fully turned on and radically present in the body can we welcome the creative "more-than" of a greater imagination . . . whether that be in art-making, lovemaking, or life-living. When we drop into the body through sensation and allow that to really open us into a sense of nothing-to-prove satiety, Eros can expand our horizons into what *could* be.

Like letting my exhaustion give way to the wonder of being fully in the magic of bathing my son or playing a silly song together. Like the way I had to drop out of my head and into my muscle memory flow with the movement of the choreography on stage. Like two lovers' disregard of embracing passion over self-consciousness. Like Ramiro's gentle instruction to stop fighting myself in my head too much, stuck in the scarcity of comparison, and instead let my body take me to a place of easeful abundance. A place in my own body that felt that I was enough, enough to feel the permission and freedom to express that enough-ness in the making of something more.

In my own life, fear tends to show up in two accusing voices in my mind: "Not enough!" and "Too much!" "Not enough" is the insecure terror that we don't have what it takes, that we are deficient, that we don't have the skills, that we don't measure up . . . that *we don't know.* It flares up like an alarm at the edge of every risk-cliff we stand on, making us question ourselves and sending us running back to the safety of what we *do* know and what feels certain.

"Too much" is the overwhelming terror that fears *we* are overwhelming or that *we will be* overwhelmed. It rises like a tide of panic that threatens to drown us or comes crashing in like a tsunami that displaces our confidence, making us feel adrift in the impossibility of being who we are in a world that has told us we must be a more manageable version to fit in, to be more *reasonable*.

These two poles of fear are often the binary one-two punch of the anxious mind in assessing the risk of the vulnerability you are stepping into as a creator/lover/human. The mind is just doing its thing, running its either/or programming. But when we forget to be here, in the body, we allow the mind to run the show, to be the only "program."

That's why we need to turn *the rest of* ourselves on.

To be turned on creatively in life, it helps to consider how we are turned on sexually. What turns you on? Whatever your kinks, it can probably be boiled down to some combination of context and being embodied and present to pleasurable sensation: touch, sight, smell, taste, and breathing. You could stay locked in your head, which would make you unavailable and not at all present to your lover. You could allow your insecurities to cause you to feel self-conscious and guarded, but then you know the sex wouldn't be very good. No. You relax the mind, relax the insecurities and thoughts that pull you out of yourself, out of the moment. You must quiet your loud thoughts by allowing the body, allowing pleasure, to take center stage. And so the very same principles that apply to arousal could be applied here to learning how to drop into embodied presence.

When I catch myself in story or in the too much / not enough spiral, I first address the context. I look to see what colors, what lines I am drawing to create the story of what is happening. I (re)member that I have a choice in what story I feed and animate: one of fear (domination) or creativity (communion). Then I try to bring my awareness to sensation in the body by focusing on my feet on the ground or my hands on my lap *through sensation.* I bring that awareness, shining it like a flashlight, and keep it there until I can feel a tingling sensation that tells me my awareness is anchoring me to those places. Then I allow that awareness to slowly lull my mind's spiraling. I allow sensation to help me relax further into my body, which, in turn, relaxes the mind.

There have been times when I will be about to record a vocal take or step on stage and I'll do this or even trail my hand in a loving caress up and down my own arm. Bringing my awareness to the sensation of touch begins a process by which I (re)member (become membered to) more of me than just my thoughts.

Touch is a quick portal for the other senses to come online and symbiotically works together with your breath. You have likely experienced aspects of the following grounding sequence without even realizing it, but I have found there is a powerful relationship between embodied sensory presence and a deepened, regulated breathing. When I feel my feet on the ground and then roll my shoulders back, for instance, I'm opening up my chest and heart (which is in and of itself a radical act of courageous vulnerability) and making more room for my breath to deepen. I let the sensation of grounded-ness, through the sensation of my feet on the ground, ground me . . . and as I relax into that grounding, I can begin to relax my stomach (usually clenched) and diaphragm. As my diaphragm relaxes, so does my throat, and so does my voice. And then from that place of feeling into my own plenitude, my own "enough-ness," I can make, which is to say, speak mindfully, listen, love, hold, empower, collaborate, cocreate something from this place of "here" into the possibility of an imaginal "there." My body is the only bridge that can make that love / idea / creative gift possible. The body is the only source of feeling connection, the only instrument that can relax into what could pleasurably become.

Tapping into a sensation is a playful erotic practice of presence. It's what allows us to feel our relatedness, our relating, as plenitude . . . as a feeling of fullness that is always available to us because we are part of it. And ironically, it is tapping into our enough-ness (plenitude) that allows for moreness (superfluity/creativity).

Embodied presence is being turned on to (be)coming together. It is being here fully, erotically enlivened so that we can create more enlivenment. It is tapping into being enough so that we can welcome more. It is about feeling satiety in the fullness of who you are so you can give more of yourself away . . . and in more and more creative ways. It is flipping the script of the domination paradigm that screams "not enough!" and "too much!" into that creative communion paradigm of "more-than-enough." And that kind of embodied presence is alluring, contagious, and sexy and will only be problematic to any system, institution, or ideology that would prefer for you to believe you're not enough or too much, and curate your identity and your creative capacity *for* you.

A turned-on embodied presence arouses us to the immediacy of an intimacy always available to us. An intimacy that is into-más-ing (into-more-ing). It's the pleasure and fullness of feeling enough—that unlocks the more than enough.

Love that keeps pouring out in a trickle of water delighting a toddler. Courage like a tiny dancer being willing to stand out. Generosity like that of the old master painter infusing his tiny students with the brilliant hue of their own capacity. Passion that discards any notion of self-consciousness. Devotion to beauty that recognizes that the true accomplishments on this earth are what we make and give away, no matter how unseen the gift or the giving may seem. It's being enough as you become more. It's the freedom of flowing with abundant life into more abundant life.

But you'll miss it. If you're not here.

Chapter Seven

For(e) Play and Multiples

The Pleasurable Trust of Creative Freedom

> *The main thing is to be moved, to love, to hope, to tremble, to live.*
>
> —Auguste Rodin

It was time. The desire had been steadily building in me for weeks, a longing I could no longer ignore. My heart steadily beating with a familiar call I recognized from childhood . . . *make me, make me, make me.* I moved the kitchen table out of the way and leaned the canvas up against the wall. I approached it as if I were approaching a stag in the wild. Cautiously and reverently. Like a prayer I didn't yet know the words for.

It had been so very long since I'd painted, now a grown woman with kids living in Michigan, and the charcoal in my hand trembled as I raised it up to the stretched canvas till it touched the surface of the textile at a singular point of contact. "YOU DON'T KNOW WHAT YOU'RE DOING!!!" my mind screamed at me.

I closed my eyes. I swear I felt Ramiro behind me. I took a deep breath, then another . . . rolling my shoulders back, relaxing my jaw, my stomach muscles. I opened my eyes on the next inhale and, with the exhale, let the line flow out of me . . . like silk. Like grace. Like love.

The next breath and the next line came easier. And the one after and the one after that, even more so. Before long, I was lost in the wordless lovemaking, charcoal dust flying into the air . . . into my hair. My body moving on its own accord, the mind lulled into peaceful surrender.

I stirred the acrylic paint and put some on my palate, saying, "Sorry I didn't mix my own like you, Ramiro" into the quiet solitude, smiling softly.

The brush tinkled gently in the water cup, like a fairy bell, like a memory. And then I began to paint. Slowly at first, and then gaining momentum. Slowing back down. Picking up speed once more. The soft hiss of brush on canvas was the only sound in my house, and I gave all of myself over to the place where two surfaces were touching, meeting, mingling, making. My body relaxed. Gaining confidence as I went that day . . . feeling into my own vulnerable longing to determine the hues of my own feelings. I felt free. So free that I ran out to get some plaster, inspired in the moment by a memory of my childhood in Spain. We used to make masks for carnival every year, lathering up our faces with thick Nivea cream and taking turns making plaster casts of our faces that we would later paint and decorate.

There was something about the memory that felt like it was part of this painting . . . a playful connection that needed making. Plaster casts heal, connect, restore. But they also are a mask, a hardening shape of a moment in time. As I cut the plaster cast up into small little pieces, the tiny grid-like texture also reminded me of the grid notebooks I grew up using in school in Spain.

I baptized the first piece, dunking it in water and carefully draining off the excess moisture, and then began adding plaster to the painting. My hands dripped with watery plaster as I smoothed each piece onto the canvas. The water dripped down my arms, the plaster caking like white mud on my fingers.

It was . . . erotic. Enthralling. Healing. Enlivening.

"Not fighting myself anymore, Ramiro," I said quietly like a declaration of love, an admission of my heart, with tears in my eyes and an impish grin he no doubt would have recognized, even all these years later.

During the pandemic, as I pivoted to becoming a full-time maker, I felt like I was dating myself . . . like there were parts of me that had gone dormant that I needed to romance and animate once more. And just as we do in our romantic relationships, I had to follow the oxygen of my instincts in seeking out this enlivenment by orienting myself to embodied presence, pleasure, and possibility. I was seducing the muse.

When we allow touch, sight, sound, and taste to become aroused, triggering the breath to deepen, it anchors us in the moment, which paradoxically opens our perception to expand into a larger imagination.

The sound of the charcoal on the canvas, the drip of the plaster as it runs down your arm, the steady rhythm of your breath, the light as it diaphanously reveals the divine hidden in each moment. The way the water hits you in the shower, the feel of the dishes in your hands, the softness of your favorite sweater, the bittersweet taste of dark chocolate on your tongue . . . everything, *everything* can become illuminated with wonder.

Letting more matter than the mind (instead of running the mind-over-matter program) helps us to relax into a noncontingent worth: a sense of our worth not reliant on a future arrival, accomplishment, approval, or achievement but rather a sense of being enough, here and now, just as we *are*. Ironically, the more present we are, the more we can create the future.

Because presence translates into pleasure and playfulness—presence is how we seduce the muse of creative possibility.

For me, it began with vintage silk kimonos. I had always been drawn to them, having received many as gifts from my Japanese boss back in Los Angeles, where I worked as a stylist at a high-end vintage clothing boutique. When I expressed my concern about appropriation to her, she spoke about paths of ensuring respect. As long as I was wearing them at home, only buying from Japanese sellers, and out of my love and respect for Japanese culture and art, she saw these as acts of reverence for the Japanese culture. That she gave them as gifts also meant she saw that respect and entrusted the gifts.

So when I found myself reaching for them instead of say, a sweatshirt, I didn't question it. I let the soft, sensual swish of fabric bring me into sensation. My reverence for the value of aesthetics in Japanese culture invited me into greater attention to my environment, texture, and the elegance of simplicity. I sat for hours playing my guitar in those silk kimonos . . . in my room, in the studio, in front of my fireplace. I wore them as I went through old photographs and a collection of old postcards and left stacks of them on my desk in my studio to draw inspiration for my songs. The kimonos became part of the silky soft admissions in the sensual play in my lyrics, in the strength of what I was discovering: soft is the hardest part.

I began to paint every day, letting the trans-verbal expression lull me into further unknowing presence . . . letting my body take over for my mind, like Ramiro taught me.

I went for walks in the woods and cared for and talked to my house plants that were steadily and surely taking over more and more real estate in my home.

I listened to records on my turntable that I hadn't listened to in years. Fleetwood Mac's *Tusk* on repeat, Neil Young's *Harvest*, Serge Gainsbourg's *L'Histoire de Melody Nelson*, and Mazzy Star's lead singer, Hope Sandoval, with her solo project *Bavarian Fruit Bread*, traveling through time with the help of sound and resonance.

I burned piñon incense, the smell bringing me back to the woods of Spain and memories of my time in New Mexico.

I laughed and played with my growing kids, in wonder at their curiosity and kindness.

I meditated, working especially with Buddhist practices of loving-kindness and compassion as I let my self-attack and critical mind relax and become more realigned with my heart.

I cooked Spanish tortillas and baked my own crusty bread that tasted like my childhood.

I boxed up "business DC Brie" attire and wore what I felt like, which was mostly vintage dresses and my old vintage Frye boots that made me feel girly and soft again, like I did when I lived in LA in my early twenties.

I lit candles, all the time . . . just like Jay did for me all those years ago in Pieholden.

I danced around my house at night when the kids were down or when I was solo and gave zero fucks about the neighbors seeing.

Finally, when the world began to reopen, I went to art exhibits . . . at any museum I could get to. I drank in the colors and the familiar landscapes of beloved artists I had reverenced in my childhood.

It was as if I was slowly and tenderly (re)membering, becoming membered once more to something vital in myself. I let all of these pieces of me come home that had felt exiled or had become fugitive from the years of heartbreak and bracing from the assault and the divorce. I nurtured the tiny flame in me that had nearly winked out from the pressures of having to "do" and "be" it all as a single mom.

Healing the relationship to my body and the sense of embodied enough-ness also healed my trust in myself . . . knowing I could trust my experience. It would be easy to gloss over that as a facile statement if not for the fact that my embodied sense of trust had been nearly shattered by the assault. When your capacity for perception has been violated, some part of you will always be left in the terrifying hall of mirrors of PTSD wondering, "Is this real? Or not real?"

Slowly, over time, that trust began to relax me into greater and greater creative confidence. I began the *Unknowing* podcast and became willing to get naked in conversation with people I admired. I was able to be courageously vulnerable precisely because I had that sense of embodied, trust-filled, relaxed presence in my enough-ness that created the supportive conditions for that disrobing.

The more I disrobed, the more I was able to touch on my authentic creative freedom and feel permission to be playful in more creative ways. I started a Patreon to share the journey of becoming a full-time maker with an alternative model of collaborative patronage. I recorded the demos that became my album *Me Veo*. I kept painting until it became clear a series was in the work, and I began selling paintings. I began developing my observations into essays that became the basis for the seasonal online courses I offered.

I seduced the muse by seducing myself . . . by making room for embodied presence, which yielded an erotic playful orientation toward creativity and possibility. The playfulness that kind of freedom elicits creates more playfulness. I guess you could say that the for(e) play is for *more* play. And the play is a seduction . . . a return to sensation, attention, and delight that blooms into a more aroused embodied experience of sensation, attention, wonder, and awe—an increase of embodied presence. This kind of erotic-creative for(e) play activates a cyclical chain reaction that renews itself over and over as you deepen:

1. Healing the relationship to your embodied self creates trust (enough-ness in the here and now, noncontingent worth).
2. Trust creates relaxation.
3. Relaxation creates confidence.

4. Confidence supports courageous vulnerability.
5. Vulnerability is the expression of authentic freedom.
6. Freedom allows for playfulness.
7. Play or playfulness invites creative permission.
8. Creative permission heals and strengthens the relationship to embodied presence (because rather than placing worth on outcomes, it returns us to the sensory simplicity of radical enough-ness in the here and now, grounded in a noncontingent worth). And the cycle begins again.

Like a dancer moving through 8-counts, you return to "one," but your body, art, expression keep moving. The erotic-creative cycle deepens, and you keep (be)coming . . . like multiples. The application of this cycling activation is useful not only in your creative projects but in your relationships too. Whether you're single, partnered, or married, all of us encounter moments of activation. Something our partner or friend says or does triggers an old ghost or old wound, and suddenly your nervous system goes into full-blown sympathetic fight or flight. You get a text from *her/him/them,* and you're so excited that your anxiety blooms, and you want to respond right away.

Your automatic reactions in this state are precisely that: automatic reactions. You don't even register what comes out of you; it just flows like lightning. *Boom.* And in the wake, you think, "Ah . . . shit. I kind of wish I hadn't scorched the earth just now with my eager excitement or intensity . . . or at the very least, responded so quickly or without thinking."

Practicing embodied presence through sensation and slowness can help in these moments. As we learn to become more present (with more than the mind), we are activating a grounded sense of noncontingent worth . . . a sense of our worthiness as *worthy just for being*, a worthiness that isn't threatened. A sense of enough-ness allows you to interact relationally from a place of deep satiety and abundance, not neediness or scarcity. So instead of reaction, we are able to act creatively in a way that is conscious, generative, and free. And that kind of spacious confidence is sexy.

The more practiced we become at tuning in to the body through sensation and activating embodied presence, the more space we develop between the situation (the stimulus, comment, offensive act, exciting text) and our response. That kind of self-soothing, grounding, embodied presence activates the exact same erotic-creative cycle in your relationships:

1. Your embodied presence helps you (re)member your inherent worthiness.
2. That trust allows you to relax your nervous system.
3. The relaxation engenders a grounded confidence (meaning a recovered sense of satiety, plenitude, abundance).
4. That confidence permits your own vulnerability (which often includes humor).
5. Your vulnerability allows you to share authentically (not combatively or anxiously).
6. That authentic freedom liberates you (and your partner) to be imperfect, to learn, and to be playful as you deepen your relationship.
7. The playfulness grants you both creative permission to try on new ways of thinking, being, loving and helps you relinquish control in favor of creativity.
8. Your shared creative permission allows you each to be more at ease to be in your body, more willing to trust the unknown, and be open to possibility, which deepens your embodied presence. And the cycle continues.

This same cycle can inform how you respond in various situations. In work, this cycle helps you touch into a grounded place in your own body that helps you feel more confident or comfortable speaking up, getting creative, or even receiving feedback in a productive way in the fourth step of simply, vulnerably making room for where you can grow, improve, learn.

This cycle is also useful in parenting. Lord knows that parenting is a daily journey over a minefield of potential activation in us as parents, so slowing down and being committed to embodied presence is what will allow for us to not be reactive, to not associate or project our worth onto our kids, and to be spacious in how we listen and support them. How we make room for them to truly be and become themselves. And at least for me, these steps represent not only the humble, creative process I want to embody or model but also the kind of present, nonanxious orientation to creative possibility I hope each of my kids will live into themselves with each problem, circumstance, and life stage they face.

It all comes back to the secret superpower we've all been given of embodied presence. Activating that first step of sensory presence and linking the relaxed embodied state with an experiential recognition of our noncontingent worth is key in activating a life of possibility, a life of creativity.

To imagine and make room for what could be, we must let go of what has been.

To let go of what has been, we must be capable of letting go . . . of not being threatened by change, by difference, by the tension-filled pressure of life as it pushes us to continue becoming.

It is a posture of experimental nonattachment. A flexible stance of humility that is okay with not knowing, with courageously moving forward into the not-yet darkness that is the womb of our might-bes. There is a beautiful Buddhist teaching and mantra that my friend Lindsay shared with me that cuts through our insecure identities, the stories we've created about ourselves and each other that keep us from being truly vulnerable, from being open to and willing to change, shift, cocreate.

Not me, not mine.

Think about how many kinds of reactive moments that statement slices through like a blade and helps you see if you are outsourcing your worth.

My art is not me; it is not mine. The moments when I'm tempted to identify with my music, my art, or whether my creativity is "succeeding" or not (whatever that means). *Not me, not mine.* How am I allowing the metrics to hijack the gift of what it means to be a maker?

My lover is not me, not mine. The moments when I'm tempted to read into a relational dynamic or a romantic disappointment. *Not me, not mine.* This lover/person is not me and not mine. Where and how am I operating from scarcity instead of plenitude, abundance, and generosity?

My kids are not me, not mine. The moments when I am exhausted as a single parent and snap in frustration at my kids because they're not doing something the way I want them to. *Not me, not mine.* Where and how am I losing touch with the wonder-filled presence that helps me recognize how precious this borrowed time with them is . . . and to grant them the permission to become who they are becoming?

In art, as in life (and in love), we can only create more art/life/love when we are present in our bodies. Where, again and again, we can remember that our worth is not contingent on what we do but rather *who we are and are becoming.* This is the freedom of radical enough-ness that grants us the trust, permission, confidence, and authenticity to play . . . to experiment . . . to create without self-consciousness, editing, or fear.

It is this kind of muscle memory of experimental nonattachment that creates grit. Resiliency is found in nonidentification because when you realize that it's not you, not yours, you are free to keep making/loving/living regardless of outcome.

Ultimately, what I am discovering in my life is precisely what Jay said to me in Pieholden when he said that "the process is the product." For me, the meaningful purpose I've been searching for my whole life, in maps and destinations, was actually right here in the present moment all along . . . in my muscles, in my breath, and in the sound of my own voice as

I give myself away, every day, and in innumerable ways. It is this deepening presence that reveals another intensity, another meaningful dimension of this life: the treasure we had in our pockets all along.

The meaning I've been searching for isn't found in knowing; it's found in *making.* Making love, art, life. Making with and giving myself collaboratively, creatively to that enlivening erotic thrum and throng all around me. And as I paint, I am praying. And when I'm cooking, I'm making love. And when I'm singing, I'm loving. And when I'm holding my kids, I am studying. And when I am doing the dishes, I am composing. Every facet of my life becomes enraptured in the singular thrall, the agony and ecstasy of this precious, fragile life, *of making more life.*

"I no longer deal in absolutes," my friend Dr. Bayo Akomolafe said to me recently. And I laughed out loud in full agreement. I no longer claim to know any certitudes about who or where or what God is, but I can say that my body resonates in recognition with the mystic Pierre Teilhard de Chardin's declaration that "[God] is . . . at the point of my pen, my pick, my paintbrush, my needle—and my heart."

Right here in my plaster-covered hands, or as my hands strum my guitar, or as my voice wanders in the dark, searching for melodies. Right here in my courage to keep going, even when I'm scared, uncomfortable, or unsure. Right here in the center of our longing, of the fires of our making, and in the throes of our becoming.

Here in that place where our *being* meets our *becoming*, where our presence welcomes a greater future, where our here-ness ushers in an unimagined there. The meaning we seek, the hope we need, the beauty that can save us is here . . . in our making.

In that "still and still moving" center of our own heart, as the poet T. S. Eliot says, as you have the courage to be present to "a deeper union, a further communion," in your courageous choice to create.

Chapter Eight

The Ache Is What Makes
Learning to Love Longing

> ***Do you think there is anything not attached by its unbreakable cord to everything else?***
>
> —Mary Oliver

"Again," she said impassively. The girls sniggered at the bar as I tried to ignore them from where I stood at the center of the studio. I began the routine, doing my best to extend and point as perfectly as I could. My arms and legs were trembling, muscles burning as I prepared for the final five fouetté turns. *First position, tendu to second position then fourth in demi plié* and I pirouetted, spun and spun, whipping my leg out perpendicularly in *développé*, down to point over my knee at plié, and back out and around each time.

"Watch your foot!" Olga yelled. "Where is your eye line?" I ended my fifth fouetté en tournant in a pitiful wobble and a half-assed croisé. "A. GAIN." She stomped her heel into the wooden floor. I wanted to scream. To cry. To yell. To run out of the studio and never come back. I was tired of being picked on, humiliated, and singled out . . . as if I weren't a full three years younger than the other girls. As if it weren't impressive that I was even at this level at my age.

I bit down every response I wanted to yell and clamped my jaw shut. Tears burned in my eyes. Hell, everything burned. I was drenched in sweat, and I was fairly certain this was the tenth consecutive time she'd asked me to repeat it.

She cued the music. I overcompensated on the third turn, throwing myself back from being so tired, and fell out.

"A . . ."

"Gain. I know." I stared at her in defiant fury.

"If you channeled half of your anger at me into your technique, we wouldn't be here."

At that, I closed my eyes. And this time . . . I went deep, deep inside me. To that place where there were no mirrors, no critical gaze of the other girls. Everything hurt. *Everything.* But I found that glowing coal at the center of me. The one that had awoken years before when I realized I *could—actually, if I wanted to—become a better dancer.* I had only been five when I lay on a mat and realized that if I chose to, I could concentrate, focus, and work to make my positions, poses, and routines better. It may seem like an obvious thing, but at five, that discovery is what resulted in my advancing quickly, skipping through class levels in the coming years.

It was the moment my longing met my agency, not that I had any of this language for it. But it was a recognition that there was deep within me a power . . . the will and capacity to change, to make, to *become.*

Exhausted and frustrated as I was, I found that burning coal deep within, and I blew on it until it became a flame. Until my heart burned as much as my muscles did. I took a deep breath and opened my eyes. And began again. It was almost unbearable. *Almost.* Like most acts of creativity.

The ache of tension burns in a similar way in me when I'm writing music. It feels like there's a molten pit between my heart and my stomach, a yearning that seems to pull songs out of me like an arrow on its way to its mark. And when I'm caught in the throes of its fury, I forget to eat . . . to think . . . I'm so consumed by the need to express this thing inside. It feels *almost unbearable.* Love is the same way. Love sets my world on fire, blinding me to anything but my lover, consuming me with desire. It is pleasure edged with pain. It is agony and ecstasy. It's *almost unbearable.*

The ache of yearning thrums through life, and on occasion we face it, we feel it . . . so acutely that it feels like we cannot bear it. We tell ourselves that this experiential intensity is a means to an end . . . that it will go away the minute we write the song, stop the stretch, have the sex, find "the one," get "the thing," scratch the itch. Basically, it will go away when we "arrive," when we are "completed" by that thing, person, achievement, status.

Most of us believe the ache of longing is for a specified completion, arrival, destination. We see the ache as a means to the relief that is hopefully at the end. We treat the ache of longing like a hot potato and are desperate to get rid of its malaise because we've been told that *longing or desire = incompleteness.*

So we rush, run, push, and pull all the strings in our power to get the guy; win the race; arrive in that position, place, or circumstance that will fulfill us and rid us from the burning ache of our desire. But if Eros is woven into the fabric of this life, then it's a little bit like telling ourselves that taking one breath once we achieve our goals will satiate our need for breathing for all time. What if the ache of longing is *always* supposed to be there? What if desire isn't a sign that we are incomplete—but is simply life's baseline?

The context for how we've been taught to think of ourselves as incomplete beings searching for our completion goes back to the time of Plato. If you're wondering where the idea of soul mates came from, you can thank Mr. P. He drafted the story blueprint that defined humanity as incomplete and separated—from our "other half," or the ultimate transcendent truth—as a way to make sense of the desire that consumed human beings.

Completion and arrival, that explains all this messy Eros and must be why our hearts are so full of longing, said Plato. And since he was a pretty influential thinker, the idea spread . . . not just in philosophy, but it became a foundational assumption of Christianity, only now it was divine completion and heavenly arrival that became the rational explanation of what we *truly* desire. That *almost unbearable* ache is just the longing to return home—away from this messy earthly reality—and be completed by God . . . one day.

Meanwhile, the idea of "soul mates" has persisted, so this, too, makes us believe that the completion and arrival we seek is *out there*, in someone else, or in following the culturally normative story that we will only be fulfilled and happy when we find "*the one*" and can be happily paired off like socks or like the animals on Noah's ark.

So whenever our bodies burn with that familiar hunger, the ache that glows like coal in your heart, the yearning for *moreness* that sparks to a flame within you. . . . we are patronizingly told, "Ah, that achy feeling? That's just because you haven't found your completion (your person, your purpose, your god) and/or destination yet."

Which then leaves us feeling . . . *torn. Split. Broken.* Like a half-soul wandering this earth, hoping we find the other half. *Incomplete.*

That *almost unbearable* ache within us gets weaponized into a story that there's something wrong with you. That you need to be fixed. The longing you feel needs to be resolved.

What if Olga had said, "That ache shouldn't be there in your muscles; dancing should resolve that feeling"? It's true that the stronger you get, the more you can move with ease, but, as any athlete knows, the ache of your muscles working and stretching *never goes away.* And yet an "out there" Completion and Arrival are still our most reached-for explanations for the ache of our longing.

We are not problematically incomplete, says Dr. Andreas Weber, not in a biological or philosophical sense. All beings in themselves are already whole because they represent a community of relationships that mutually supports your collective selfhood. These relationships aren't "halves" searching for another half . . . they are a many-ness always creating a moreness. Completion is not that goal; creativity is.

If we're not *incomplete*, then perhaps the ache of our longing is not the desire for completion but something else entirely. Could it be that Eros throbs, not as an ache for certain/specific outcomes . . . but as *the* ache that fuels our creativity, our becoming? A fullness never arrived at. An ending never finalized. A door always left open. The reality of a world that is contingent on continuing in unknowing, in uncertainty, because this is the fundamental necessity for imagination, creativity, and more life to flow.

Completion is a myth. What we are actually longing for is not on the other side of change but change itself . . . to be transformed. To touch and be touched. To affect and be affected. To resound and to resonate. To love and be loved. To deepen, to reconsider, to be surprised, to be astonished. To be left not with answers but with a question. And then another. And then another. And this is not an enclosed arrival but rather an insatiable hunger for moreness, which is the creative impetus. Which is life. Which is love.

In the Erotic worldview of abundance, desire is not the scarcity of grasping *for a thing, person, or destination*. Desire is the foundational feeling-ness of life. It's the ache that makes. The yearning is not hijacked into the completion myth of the domination paradigm ("if you have this/them, you'll be happy."), but rather it is the superfluous plenitude that creates *more* possibility ("if you befriend this achy feeling, you'll make, expand, grow, transform into more"). The Completion myth makes you believe the solution is found "out there" somewhere (in another person, in having something, in reaching a desired destination). The Erotic Creative experiences a pleasurable fulfillment "here and now" in the body, in the present moment, which allows for a creative moreness to infuse everything we do . . . and instead of believing our happiness is in the future, we feel joy now. *Because the process is the product.*

When that kind of erotic luscious, languid, and unhurried creative delight gets turned on in you, you'll be liberated from not only the myth of incompletion but the myth of arrival as well.

If you've ever wondered why some of the world's most accomplished people seem so unsatisfied, it's because they've believed the arrival myth hook, line, and sinker. No matter what peak or zenith of achievement, success, or financial gain they reach in this life, there is a manic, panicky obsession with a larger achievement, success, or financial gain. "Never enough!" cries the hoarding scarcity of fear in the domination paradigm that espouses the insecurity driving this type of ambition. And because it's never enough, they are secretly depressed. Winning at the domination game but losing the secret of abundant joy and pleasurable plenitude along the way.

The secret has been right there all along: You are not incomplete, and there is no destination you need to arrive at in order to feel fulfilled. Fulfillment is found when you make *making* (learning, growing, giving) the focus of the *aching* you feel. When the product becomes the process.

But how do we befriend that ache of our longing as not being about a desired outcome? How do we accept yearning as foundational?

When you're wrapped up in the passionate throes of having sex with your lover, the tension you are seeking release for, in both your partner and in yourself, is not something you're mistaking as final. Intuitively you know that your longing will only open deeper and deeper levels of intimacy, of connection and creative possibility . . . so instead of thinking of that burning tension as a problem to be solved, you embrace it as feeling that *creates.* You allow yourself to feel the anguish of all that longing then because you're not running from it. You recognize the ache as what makes, as what is driving your love. The more you give, the more you receive. Desire becomes a drive of abundant creativity.

In creativity, this switch from mistaking your longing as being about completion or arrival instead of the pleasurable ache of creative drive is the same.

As an artist, I feel far freer to express myself playfully and in every possible way when I'm not confusing my longing (my purpose in creating) for any achievement or destination but rather when I allow it to be an end unto itself . . . when I see it as the desire to keep making more—more life, more art, more love. I let the process become the product. I slow down enough to feel the pleasure of being a maker. Suddenly I feel deep satisfaction in what I am making. I am fulfilled, enlivened, and animated to keep making. Not for the sake of completion or arrival but for the sake of creating itself.

Those years in ballet taught me how to make peace with that ache and feel it . . . not as a problem to be solved but as the fundamental tension of this life. To see the ache as part of the matrix of this planet. To breathe, to notice through sensation what it feels like and where . . . and allow the body to ground the experience and help us unhook it from the story we've created about it or from the craving to turn it into control over a person, circumstance, or situation to meet our own expectations or projections. And when we do, we are befriending the ache . . . allowing it to move in us and through us on its creative path to moreness . . . even when its path to moreness involves heartbreak or loss.

When I went through a particularly brutal heartbreak, it felt *almost unbearable.* I felt lost in a hall of mirrors that kept shattering into sharp edges that cut me the more I tried to pick up the fragments, the more I tried to rationalize the devastation I felt. Even though the relationship had run its course, everything in my body wanted immediate relief . . . to fix and resolve it. Perhaps you can recall the way the ground gives out beneath you with unexpected heartbreak or the loss of a loved one . . . how the cavernous gap they left rips open your soul. How your voice seems to echo within the loss as a mocking reminder that they are gone, but you call out for them anyway. And your call becomes a keening song until only silence remains.

The ache of heartbreak cuts deep and in some cases, never goes away. But even this ache can be understood as love. As an ache that makes. Because ultimately, that is what life and love do . . . they keep making. Even when our hearts are shattered, through time, we are remade into a new shape . . . not despite the fissures but precisely because of them.

In the end, "every separation is a link," says Simone Weil. The changes and the losses only reveal the preciousness of what was shared. The ache that runs through everything is an ache of love. Whether the separation is of a teacher and student, parent and child, lover and beloved, or a person and a place. To stop our restless running, our compulsive distractions, and quietly turn within to face that great ache is to accept the inherent separation of life in death, to recognize that consciously *bearing the ache* and letting go is an utmost precious act of love. So even when we are grieving loss, we can turn toward that ache and recognize that the pain we feel is because *love made a bond* . . . and even when some relationships end, that bond gifts us with transformation, with change, with growth. Nothing is wasted or lost. Not ever. Every single offering you have given and received in the exchange of love lives on forever in the unseen artery of this cosmos in the heart of the universe. Every single offering you have given and received in love lives on in your own beating and expanding heart, made more tender and more alive by your willingness to *feel*.

The ache you feel burning in your chest even now is Eros, is love . . . the thread that runs through everything in this material plane. It is the beams we must bear in recognizing that only love can speak flesh and matter into existence as unutterably precious, precisely because it is fragile and passing. Everything changes. And it is hard to bear that changeability, the decay, the loss of what has been. But this is the great secret: only through letting go can we "let be"—and allow life-force (creativity) to make something new in the ashes of what has been. Ecologically, this is our great homecoming to our place in the family of everything. It is to (re)member ourselves as fragile, decaying, renewing, complexifying, dying, and trying to live *anyway* just as all life is on this planet.

When you can accept that the ache you feel *is* the love, it changes our reptilian brain's reaction to reject the ache we feel. We can soften our bodies in an exhale of surrendered acceptance, which is to say: we can finally stop resisting it and instead feel it deeply and allow it to run its course through us . . . changing us as it does.

Looking back over your life, did the ache of Love not change you, transform you, or help you grow in some way? Did it not reveal a story you had held or expand you into broader horizons? Did Love not disclose its secret that it's precisely through the ache that it is making something new?

The ache is what makes. The act of actually getting stronger hurts. We all know this when it comes to building muscle but don't apply the same principle to growth, creativity, or transformation.

I'm no longer assigning any type of completion or satiety in a person, project, or outcome. What that kind of shift away from the maps of external completion and "one day" arrival provides is freedom. Believing myself already complete and already arrived (here and now) liberates me to create from plenitude and generous abundance. It frees me to make, live, and love freely.

And as I've worked to embrace the ache of life, it has freed me to realize that my experience of longing—when I really am present to what is beneath it all—isn't about *someone* or any type of approval or achievement. It's just the hunger pang I feel in me *to keep going deeper into Unknowing* and to *make.* It's the burning desire of life itself on the way to more life. It's the pleasurable ache of Love itself seducing me further into more Love.

The more we choose back the tenderness of feeling that ache, the more we can create. When it's no longer about completion or arrival, the ache of being a maker makes us more sensitive, perceptive, attentive, attuned. It teaches us to feel it all through vulnerable sensitivity, and it's precisely that sensitivity to what is precious about this life that helps others see it too.

The ache is what makes us tender enough to perceive the beauty and wonder all around us.

The way the old couple walks slowly down the park lane holding hands. The startling laughter of a child. The bloom of a rose on a trellis. The powerlessness and heartbreak in the face of war or tragedy and the fragility of life that it forces us to reckon with. The light on the lake. The wounds you couldn't avoid. The small, stubborn shoot growing through the concrete cracks anyway. The way things always change.

The ache opens us into a greater acceptance of how ephemeral everything is and, by that fact, appreciating how beautiful this life is.

Sometimes I feel beauty so acutely, it hurts . . . it breaks my heart. And I let it. I let it. There are so many moments when I think I can't bear it. When the days of solo parenting and the risk of being a creative feel too much.

And with every fissure of my heart, of my willingness to feel, I become more tender, more willing to accept life on its own terms instead of trying to control it. With each crack, I'm able to let more in and more of me out. Which means I feel more and more alive the more vulnerable I become.

The ache is what makes. So stop running from it, stop resisting the very fragility that makes us permeable. The very hunger that drives our yearning . . . that flares up in us like a sun star, pulls us like gravity into an almost-crushing embrace. A grounding force that moves us to touch and be touched. To transform and be transformed. So let it.

The ache is what makes. And it is almost unbearable.

Almost.

Chapter Nine

La Petite Mort
The Orgasmic Little Deaths

The creative process is a process of surrender, not control.

—Bruce Lee

I dramatically slid before the dining room mirror, imagining the spotlight hitting me just as the drums came in. I sang the opening line into the wooden spoon—I mean, mic—along with Robyn's "Dancing on My Own" blasting through my house.

I dragged my hand up my leg and popped my hip while singing the next line. Then I threw my ass around as I pivot-turned down the hall . . . I mean, stage. The audience (no one) was going wild.

I pirouetted in my socks and landed right on cue in a power stance, not caring that I was a walking millennial white woman cliché as I threw my head back and sang loudly out of tune. I pantomimed the anguish as I danced . . . my ponytail whipping around. Now I was really going for it. I turned, eyes closed in front of my bay windows (thank God the blinds were down), and opened my eyes for the finale, belting the triumphant anthemic line:

"*I keep dancing on my . . .*" *ooo*h fuck.

Blinds NOT down. Definitely not down at all as the word died on my lips and I stared open-mouthed at my neighbor six feet from me on the other side of the window, where his dog was taking a shit on my lawn and where he had, I realized to my mortification, totally witnessed this whole entire performance. I waved with a half smile frozen on my very red face and let the earth swallow me whole. He laughed and picked up his dog's shit and went on his way. And as soon as he turned, I lowered the blinds.

I wish I could say that's the only time that ever happened. At this point, I'm the fully functioning comedic shit-show-single-mom-working-artist foil to my neighbors' Mayberry lives. I might as well keep them entertained. Being an artist often feels like you're dancing on your own at night and everyone you know is watching through the window. It's brutal. And . . . I *hate* feeling vulnerable.

This may come as a surprise, given all that I've vulnerably shared in this book and on a podcast that millions have listened to or because I'm a musician and artist who has put myself in front of the public by way of song, art, image, and word just about every other day. But being in front of a microphone, camera, or behind the guitar on a stage for me is the equivalent of a well-fitting piece of armor or breastplate. Some part of me feels protected by the distance of a recording, by the elevation of the stage, by hiding behind my instrument.

But the minute I release a recording, publish a piece, or finish a painting, I'm a fucking mess. I pace my house like a caged wildcat. I cry. I stress eat. I lash out like the caged wildcat. I cry again.

This postpartum malaise usually lasts a day. But, man, what a day.

I and the people in my life have a shorthand for these days: Release Melt-Down Day. We've all gotten so good at weathering it that plenty of space is given for the wildcat pacing, tissues handed out for all the tears, and ample distancing from the sharp claws. Now I can even laugh about it in the moment, and the laughter helps me get softer toward myself in compassion.

Soft is the hardest part of being vulnerable. And staying soft is the hardest part about being a maker/lover/human.

While I can open myself and metaphorically disrobe before an audience, put me in front of one man who is pursuing me romantically, and I'm as spooked as a wild deer in the forest. Or as suspicious and self-protective as a she-wolf. Or as edgy as a pufferfish. Or some weird alien combination of the three. Pufferdeer Wolfish. That's me. That's how I truly get about letting someone in, romantically, which may explain why I'm still single. Remember the miles of enchanted thickets in Disney's *Sleeping Beauty*? Combine those with the booby traps of Indiana Jones's *Raiders of the Lost Ark*, and you're vibing the terrain around my heart. The fact that a few managed to slip in past the first several moats and death traps over the last few years at all is a miracle.

I've clearly been through some things and have compassion for my body's initial instincts. Trauma and heartbreak and having to be a keep-everything-going-and-together single mom can make it difficult to be soft. It takes time romantically to truly gauge someone's character, their consistency, their trustworthiness. Vulnerability is a slow, uncomfortable stretch . . . a willing disrobing into revealing the fleshy, unarmored core. And yet . . . I know no other way, no other direction, than to keep opening: song by song, thought by thought, story by story, and (reluctantly) date by date in a perpetual trust fall sans armor. And the thing is, this particular sacred exchange is just not a one-and-done thing.

We all armor up again and again, often without consciously being aware of it, and only come to realize it when our creativity, growth, or life-force is asking us to hand it over. I picture us looking at the scene in surprise: "Oh shit! Ha . . . uh . . . how'd that get there again??" I have a crap ton of armor designed in every color and for every season, mostly editions of "stay away, please, thank you."

What I've had to make peace with is that, one by one, I'll be asked to hand the protective armor over, again and again and again. I'll eventually get naked. I'll step from behind the mic, guitar, canvas. I'll let go of outcomes as I get vulnerable with the world, again and again . . . because that is the call of the creative. Everyone is included in that category. All of us are all asked to remove our self-created invulnerable covering because ultimately what we are hiding behind *is what keeps us from really being seen.*

True courageous creativity happens when we trade that hard metal armor for our soft, fleshy, undefended selves. Our true selves. The selves that have nothing to prove, no false bravado, the ones who learn how to become comfortable in the discomfort of being vulnerable. Intimacy will always require vulnerability, and intimacy will always challenge the ways the ego resists it.

To me, despair is what happens when we wear our armor so long that it becomes inextricable from our flesh . . . and little by little, we cut ourselves off from our hearts, from feeling, from exposing our hearts to the world, armoring up against touch, softness, pleasure, and hope. When we become so rusty and rigid and afraid of failure that we never risk anything at all . . . and we stop being makers. Isolated and convinced that our control and self-protection are good things, we're surprised when despair begins to slowly take over like the strange sleep of hypothermia. Little by little, we go numb and are lulled into a dangerously mortal sleep.

The exposure and little deaths we experience when we become vulnerable as creators/lovers/humans is nothing compared with the slow death of despair we risk if we don't.

Ultimately, you have to want to experience the life fully alive more than your desire to self-protect from the possibility of pain.

And that tenet applies to creativity as well. Because as every mother knows, giving birth isn't exactly a cakewalk . . . but what gets us through the contractions is the desire to hold that little person we've been waiting to meet. And that desire is so much greater than the pain . . . because we know the joy of holding that precious new life will eclipse everything before it.

New life always demands vulnerability. Whether that new life is love, creativity, a project, a bold move, or an act of courage. You have to be present, soften, and open. You have to feel your heart. Every beat. In the unforgiving morning light, it's never easy to be totally naked—let's be real. Even so, this erotic sacred exchange . . . costly as it is . . . is always, *always*, worth it. And it hinges on our *choice* to say yes.

The temptation within us to armor up in self-protection is a constant. Most of us don't even realize we're doing it. We fall into that mind-over-matter thing where we cling to our stories and identities like helmets and shields and then wonder why we feel so disconnected, so alone.

Remember, the mind can only do the ones and zeros programming of dualisms, of comparison, of grand stories with villains and heroes. The mind is the realm of the ego, with its fragile self-protection and need for validation and approval. So what happens when we courageously risk, create, love? We move against that armored instinct. We put the armor down and take off all that hinders our movement.

Instead of mind-over-matter, we discover that there is more that matters than the mind's (or ego's) version of reality. It will kind of feel like you're dying. Because your ego *is* dying a little. Because you're willing to let others see you, feel you, taste you as real . . . as imperfectly perfect, as not in control, as unknowing. As *vulnerable.*

The mind, the ego, wants to maintain control, power-over, and prop itself up. It wants to remain invulnerable. Why? Because it is the part of us that is afraid. This is why we shame-spiral when we don't feel we performed as well during that show, that meeting. When we mess up and hit the wrong pedal or say the wrong thing or make mistakes. Our ego can't take the threat to the carefully curated image of ourselves that we are trying to present to the world. It prefers the two-dimensional filtered avatar version of us, not the fleshy, real, feeling, and flawed version of us.

The ego is the part of us that is quite simply afraid. Because of that, I'm not into approaching the ego with spiritually lofty or violent plans of annihilation. That doesn't work. No part of us deserves that kind of dominant energy. Instead, a more loving approach of ego-integration helps the ego relax into recognizing and harmonizing with the full self. Like the string of a guitar that is tuned too sharp, the ego can be tuned to a more harmonic frequency of a loving desire to cocreate. As you ease that fear and (re)member a larger sense of self (become membered to a more embodied and interconnected self), you are able to be vulnerable, curious, and creative. You are able to move from the power-over control of the ego to the creative power-with of love. So, instead of operating out the tyranny of propping up an identity or armored personality, we become free persons, cocreating and being created into something new all the time.

The relief of softness happens when we can finally laugh at ourselves, at how hard we fight vulnerability . . . at how much we try to armor up against letting ourselves simply be fleshy, soft, human.

When we soften in this unarmored, undefended way, our will becomes creatively fluid as power-with *willingness* rather than calcified by insistence, or the controlling power-over of *willfulness*. And as we soften our willfulness into willingness, the focus of our longing shifts from *craving* (possessing or having) to *creating* (giving).

Eros is the fuel of desire: the energy flow of longing that seeks connection and creation. So when our desire is misaligned, it will not only show up in the quality of what we make but immediately give itself away in our bodies. Egoic willfulness shows up in the hunch of your shoulders, in the pitch of your voice as it becomes shrill and thin in your defensiveness, in the set of your jaw in your judgment, in the roll of your eyes of your dismissal. When your energy is so busy defending your fragile ego with armored power-over moves, there's little space for Eros to move in and through you.

This is why embodiment, and the capacity to self-regulate so we can be attuned and attentive to sensations happening in the body, is so important. The body will tell you when the ego is flaring up. Our bodies are a symphonic whole that only feel pleasurably enlivened when Eros is flowing in and through us in orchestrated power-with. When we flip into the craving of power-over, it will immediately show up as dysregulation of our body's creative circuitry. You feel it immediately as disembodied disconnection.

When your desire is coopted and driven by wanting to prove, wanting to have, possess, or control (manipulate), that is egoic craving. Craving will link arms with the fear of "too much / not enough" and seductively disconnect you from your own body's inherent presence, your sense of radical enough-ness and belonging. Craving will whisper to you in a way that creates entitlement and envy via comparisons . . . that *you* deserve what they have, you *should* have their opportunities, you *should* be up on that stage getting that award, attention, spotlight. Craving will make your creativity about arrival points, about *having*. So, ironically, in the effort of having and possessing, you will lose yourself.

You could picture ego-craving as Gollum, the former hobbit turned hideous creature in *The Lord of the Rings* by his obsession with the ring of power, which he referred to as "Mine, my own . . . my precious."

Once possessing becomes your motive, your noncontingent self has been outsourced to the object of your craving. If your rootedness has been outsourced, then your vision of possibility is compromised. Instead of the wide imaginal vision of creative possibility, you have tunnel vision for the only outcome you've convinced yourself is the one that must happen. With your vision and trust inverted, your authenticity/voice, heart, and creative engine are on borrowed time. Soon they, too, will start to flicker out . . . one by one. You will burn out. You will feel empty. You will feel dead inside. You'll be Gollum.

The difference between craving and the creative true self, believe it or not, is our ability to yield control. Control of the narrative, of the outcome, of the hoped-for result. Unknowing becomes a conscious act of surrender, of yielding our hope in a humble posture of cooperation and collaboration with life on its way to more life. It is the radical choice to relax the ego and the mind and come back into full co-creative presence and let things simply be . . . so that more can come.

By the way, it's that exact same relaxation and unarmored vulnerability that makes sex pleasurable.

In the best passionate throes of doing and being done unto, of devouring and being devoured, of being two and dissolving into one, there is a constant dance of leading the loving and conscious surrender in being loved . . . that climaxes into a shared conscious surrender.

You're like . . . yeah, but that's sex. Letting go of my self-protection and letting go of outcomes or letting people truly see me as I am creatively and relationally is like watching my ego cry out, "I'm melting! I'm mellllting!!!" Wicked-Witch-of-the-West style. It feels like *dying.*

Yes, yes, it does. But it is a death that yields an increase in life as it is composted. It is a conscious, surrendered dying that opens us up to more possibility, creativity, life, and moreness. Perhaps this is why the French euphemism for orgasm is *la petite mort*. . . . "little death."

The ultimate release into orgasm is a letting go of control, a surrender into the other, a small death of sorts. In sex and life and creativity, Eros moves in and through the following progression: Frustration breeds creativity. It is a frictional force that builds the heat. The creative act is a move toward frustration, not away. The tension begins to build and mount. You're invited to take both active and passive roles, giver and receiver, assertive and vulnerable. And then . . . a conscious yielding leads to a surrender of ecstasy, of more-than-you-ness.

Being undone is part of being vulnerable.

The unmaking in life is the making of life.
The unmaking in love is the making of love.
The unmaking in creativity is the making of creativity.

The unmaking is the making.

This is hot shit. And maybe by framing it in sexual language, you can feel into the ways that letting go of the egoic self-protection isn't all death and dying in some sort of spiritual self-flagellation of perfection. We love our ego back into membership with the rest of us so we can love more . . . and as we relax that instinct to self-protect or hide, we realize it's actually pleasurable to let it go.

Power *with*. Willingness. Conscious surrender.

Feel into the ways your body naturally understands this erotic invitation better than your mind. How could this not teach us that conscious surrender is the seed of life's pleasure? How could this not help us see that yielded receptivity to the waves of possibility will always carry us to new heights? It's also the way of intimacy . . . of letting someone see us as we are, with all our quirks and nonfiltered faces, gravity-bound and stretch-marked.

In the end, the little deaths can teach us that surrender (even when it's painful or hard) and acceptance can lead to more life, new life, to a pleasure-filled *yes*! And sometimes the petite mort of yielding control and vulnerable surrender is hardest to do when life offers us something that feels too good to be true. Sometimes it's the gifts of this life that we resist the most in fear. Sometimes it's hardest to take the armor off to let love *in*.

A couple of years ago, I got an unexpected phone call from a former colleague. Within minutes, he explained that he had an unexpected opportunity for me in the form of an all-expenses-covered trip to join a small group of dreamers and doers on a small island in Central America.

My response was not immediately "hell, yes!" I asked a billion questions, most of which he didn't have answers for. Who was going to be there? He didn't know. What would we be doing? He wouldn't say. Also, the trip was in four days. I had planned on being in New York City over the weekend, so I could leave from there, but it all just felt so wild. Spontaneous. Weirdly wonderful, yes . . . but we've been well groomed to be suspicious of wonderful things. I haven't done "wild," "spontaneous," or experienced a whole lot of "weirdly wonderful" since becoming divorced and carrying the weight of single-parenting with a whole lot of sacrifice, work, and worry.

It's weird how we even become identified with our own challenges or hardships. *I'm a single mom . . . I don't get to do last-minute fun things!* I'm quite used to my heavy-ass, rusty armor, thank you very much. There were a billion reasons to say no. As I shared this all with my kids, it was my then twelve-year-old who looked at me and said, "Mom, this sounds like an adventure of a lifetime. Just say YES!"

While it took me employing just about all my unknowing tools, I did. I didn't know a damn soul on the trip and had absolutely no idea if I was going to be tricked into being a drug mule, end up stuck in some sort of weird psychedelic retreat, or be recruited into a cult. I felt vulnerable in every way. But I trusted my instincts (and my son's) and said YES.

What ensued were four of the most magical, heart-expanding, deeply bonding, and unforgettable days of my life . . . and I now consider the people I met on that trip family. In one of the most magical moments of the trip, I rope-climbed up to the top of the jungle canopy by myself, and while I was up there, I recovered a part of myself I thought I had nearly lost: the wild one, the one that says YES, the girl who jumps off cliffs and into every body of water, the one who is first in line to rope-climb and dive into any adventure. The insatiable lover in me . . . the one who is unafraid of vulnerability and sees it as fecund potentiality. The woman who can consciously surrender in playful creativity and in steadfast trust that something is seductively calling me out of "what has been" into the wild wonderful of "what could be." Letting go of control, knowing, or any sense of certainty was a "little death." A risk-filled, embodied, conscious surrender into a pleasurable *more* that I could never have imagined.

Sometimes conscious surrender is being willing to embrace the adventure of what is almost too good to be true . . . but, like sex, our embodied capacity to be fully present, tuned in, and turned on will enable a generous, creative, and life-engendering pleasure. Some part of us resists believing, trusting, or accepting the gift. But what if every magical experience/truth/revelation is just waiting for our courage to believe we are worthy of it?

What awaits you on the other side of your little deaths?

What awaits you on the other side of your willingness to say and embody your *YES?*

Pleasure. Possibility. Relationships. Creativity. Everything.

Chapter Ten

Tied Up and Constraints
What If This Isn't a Problem?

Art lives from constraints and dies from freedom.

—Leonardo da Vinci

"Check, one . . . one, two . . ." I messed with my levels a little more, trying to find that sweet spot for my mic signal. Once I had gotten it just right, I started playing the instrumental track and hit record on my vocal. I took a deep breath, opened my mouth to sing my first line, and . . .

"MOOOOOM! MAMAMAMA!" *You've got to be kidding me.* I had literally just gotten both kids down for a nap. I threw my headphones off, nearly tripping on my mic cable as I hurried out to Søren's room before his bellowing woke up Rowan. "MOOOOOOMMMMMY!!"

"Shhhh . . . I'm coming. I'm coming, baby. I'm here, shhhh, quiet," I whispered as I rushed into the dark room.

"Mommy, I had a nice sweepies!" my little thunder said cheerfully from his bed.

"No, no, honey, you didn't. I just walked out, like, five minutes ago."

"I did! I DID! I HAD A NICE SWEEPIES!!!" He began melting down. I picked him up and held him. "Søren, honey, it's time for a nap now." *One that is decidedly longer than five minutes.* "Mama will hold you for a little bit, and then it's time for sleepies, okay?"

"Okay," he conceded tearfully, nuzzling his face into my neck and clasping his arms tightly around my shoulders. I leaned my cheek on his wild mop of hair as I rubbed his back. "Sowen's song?" His little muffled request tugged at my heart, and I began singing.

I know a boy with a name like thunder…
Rolling across the desert plane,
Eyes like the sea in stormy wonder,
Shaking down the barley grain.

His little voice joined in, making up Søren-babble for the words he couldn't say. I don't even remember when I wrote the song or what it means really. I just know it became real one day and then became more real with every utterance. Like a spell. Like a prayer.

Who can know the paths he'll take to?
Ides and years they cannot claim,
My little boy with a name like thunder,
He's shaking down the barley grain,
He's shaking down the barley grain.

By the last line, Søren had stopped singing. I carefully laid him down and tiptoed out of the room. Thanking all the gods for the fact that Ro had slept through his brother's attempt at nap mutiny, I snuck back into the tiny study. Okay, where was I? Oh, yeah, the first line. I backed the track up, hit record, and started singing.

Looking back on those years when the kids were little, life was marked by constant interruptions, lack of sleep, and no autonomy over my days. Every day was an unknowing, and there was no way to anticipate if I'd have space to shower, let alone record, write, or read. Some days I would get lucky and literally record demos one line at a time, in ten-minute intervals between the kids' nap resistance. Most days, I simply surrendered to the flow of their needs, of playing hours of the same game on the floor, daily walks outside regardless of the weather, of messes and stains everywhere . . . constant diapers and potty times, tears and giggles. It was wonder-full, and it was hard as hell.

Though I was married then, I felt completely alone. Left to grapple with the reality that my job as a creative didn't include an office to go to, and even though we couldn't afford day care, I didn't want to miss that window with the boys anyway. I felt—and in so many ways *was*—torn. But I stubbornly held on to the contrasting notes of musician and mother, willing them to harmonize. I let love make a blender of my life, throwing my moments of creative expression in the mix with the demands of being a mother to two creatures under the age of three, and sometimes the smoothie was good, and sometimes it was crap (literally). And the thing is, looking back, I wouldn't trade those years for all the unhurried and uninterrupted time in the world.

The difficulty experienced when life imposes a constraint on our lives is that some part of us rebels, thinking, "Wait, I didn't sign up for this!" Even when it's miraculous like becoming a parent, suddenly the life we had before kids disappears into a fog of a hazy ambiguous glow of "before" (what *did* we do with all that time?) as we reckon with the pressing demands of the "after." It's the feeling we have in the dead of winter when we can't remember what summer feels like (*was it really warm enough to be out in shorts? Really?*). At least this is winter-true for those of us who live in Michigan.

Living in Michigan is to be forced to make peace with the extremes. Winter comes earlier and stays longer here. For many years, I (along with most) bitterly complained my way through this season . . . bemoaning the seemingly endless months on end of gray. But somewhere along the way, I decided I was tired of dreading it. Tired of complaining. Tired of pissing and moaning about it. So . . . I stopped. I equipped myself with better winter gear, filling my house with candles and twinkle lights, and got outside as often as possible. I decided to befriend it. And the most magical thing happened. I began to appreciate it.

Constraints are part of life. Something, a literal or figurative winter, will force you to reckon with limitations. The point is, the winter season in your creative cycle will and must come . . . whether it's a season of feeling like your creativity has just disappeared under the ice or whether you suddenly find yourself in a blizzard of larger demands that force you to compress your creative expressions in tiny, borrowed moments. In those times, we have a tendency to think that whatever season we are in is what *it will always be like.*

Instead of resisting creative winters (trying to have power over it), we find the creative gift when we work with the limitations (power with). This is a radical reframing of how you likely initially react when your creativity goes quiet, when your energy is hibernating under a heavy blanket of snow. This is also not how we've been taught to look at seasons of circumstantial constraints like parenting little ones, caring for an aging parent, loss, grief, or any other unknowing. We have been taught to resist and "power-through" constraints by the hangover of industrialization that has disconnected us from seasonality, by electricity that has unplugged us from daily rhythms, by technology that has logged us off from healthy boundaries. We have been conditioned to never, never, ever, be "OFF." Never not be okay. Never not be "fine." Never not be producing. We have become so identified with "productivity" as a metric for our being accepted and finding belonging that our first question when we meet someone new is "what do you do?"

Modernity has made us feel that we should be ashamed when we simply cannot force ourselves to produce or barrel past the grief that is lovingly begging you to slow down. If you can't "fake it till you make it" or feel embarrassed because the way you pay your bills and your creative passions are not currently the same thing, you probably think it's your fault. That you missed the boat somehow. That you missed a page, a stage, or a step in the how-to-live-properly book. *That there's something wrong with you.*

But what if there is nothing wrong with you? What if this or any seasonal hush, full stop, quieting in our creative and yearly life cycle isn't a problem?

What if the problem is simply our relationship to the cyclical nature of life and our general malaise with winter seasons requiring us to relinquish control? What would happen, I wonder, if we were to cease the colonializing instinct to conquer, force, and indenture our creative life-force/energy? What would happen if we were to flip the complaint of seasons of darkness, cold, and quiet into curiosity? What if we were to turn inwardly and hold all that cannot be fully captured in words or ideas in a tender, loving womb?

We got stuck in the evolutionary assumption that warm is good, cold is bad. Dominated by the world of labels and identifications that prolific productivity is "success" and going still, quiet, or receptive is "failure." Each of these learned beliefs creates a dichotomy that separates us, our reality, and our own lives and life cycles into judgments that make us feel more divided, disconnected, and disassociated from our bodies, each other, and the environment.

A radically different posture to live into is curiosity: seeking to understand and respect the relationship between ourselves and the other (whether that other is a person, a circumstance, an animal, a rock formation, a season, an environment). Rather than beginning from a place of separateness (you do you), curiosity assumes relationship, connectedness, interdependence. And because of that, it assumes responsibility.

Curiosity begins the process of shifting our perspective from one of power-over to power-with. Those gray skies that everyone here in Michigan loves to complain about? They exist because of our proximity to the Great Lakes. It's called "the lake effect." Condensation rises off the lakes, and because of the sun's lower position, condensation is horizontally stratified, resulting in widespread and longer-lasting overcast skies. In a world that is *literally* on fire, those gray skies are a beacon of life, a signal of the gift a glacier left behind in the form of huge reserves of fresh water in the middle of this country. Those lakes may one day save lives. Now when I look up and see gray, I'm not complaining. I'm grateful. That gratitude translates to a sense of appreciation, care, and concern toward this place I call home. I won't sit here and complain about winters in an environment that may one day become one of the last vestiges capable of thriving life in North America.

The creative opportunity that exists when life hands you a new set of circumstantial constraints is discovered only when you *choose it back*. When you say, "Okay, I didn't initially choose this . . . I didn't ask for my life to suddenly be hemmed in by xyz, but I'm going to trust that this constraint can be a creative womb (not a tomb)."

During those early years as a young mom, I fell in love with mystics across several traditions, these wild souls whose embodied experience of the divine transcended (and often threatened) the religious institutions they were in. So I began studying the mystical streams of Christianity and Sufism, as well as dipping into Buddhism. I started meditating and got up at five-thirty (like you do) just so I could have some time to read and meditate before the boys woke up.

I would get up, make coffee, sit down, and—much like my demo making during those days—I would undoubtedly be ten minutes into my meditation when one of the boys would wake up. It didn't matter if I got up earlier, either. They just seemed to have a homing beacon that knew when I was finally doing something (anything) that I wanted to do.

When I enrolled in a two-year formation program on mysticism through the Center for Action and Contemplation, I complained about this to one of the faculty, James Finley. "Jim, meditation and all this oneness and transcendence and hours of prayer and meditation sounds great, really it does," I said, "but it feels like it's apparently only available and reserved for folks who are retired and have nothing else to do with their time. Where is the mystic with one screaming babe on her hip, another screaming toddler at her feet while she's trying to type on her laptop while the dinner is burning on the stove? Because that is MY life."

He gave one of his mischievous smiles and said, "Okay, okay . . . let's role play this moment. You be you, and I'll be God or transcendent Love."

"Alright," I said, quirking up one brow cynically.

"Now, Brie, I can't tell you what it means to me that you're getting up to meditate and commune with me every morning. And I'm sitting there with you, and we're sitting in that center of love together and honestly . . . it moves me to tears. I mean, look at you—you're so tired, but you're still getting up *so* early . . . you're giving up sleep for me, and really that just moves me so much." We all kind of chuckled at this Jim-God-Love impersonation.

And then he looked at me under his big, bushy eyebrows with a twinkle in his eye. "But you see, the thing is, I'm so moved by you that I just can't handle it, so I rush into the bodies of your children, and I wake them up because I want to know what it's like to be held by *you*."

Holy shit, what a reframe, I thought as tears filled my eyes and streamed down my face. And I wasn't alone. There wasn't a dry eye in that hall.

Whatever the set of constraints in your life, what if it isn't a problem? What if the interruptions of your life are actually God, Source, Love, the universe . . . rushing in to touch and be touched by you, to interact with you, to cocreate with you? The surrendered stance I took as a young mother (albeit exhausted and not without moments of deep, real angst and frustration) was to simply practice allowing my creativity to exist *within and as* the shape of my life. Instead of seeing those demanding days as a problem, I chose to embrace the constraints as part of the womb that was creating something new in my life. As a season that was engendering something vital in me, something new, even in all the pressure I felt in that womb.

Another way to look at it is the playful erotic stance of consent to ties and constraints. Being tied up immediately connotes loss of control, of being made powerless . . . and in so many ways, the circumstantial constraints of life do this to us. But when—in loving playfulness—we choose them back, the ties suddenly go from a symbol of a lack of agency to becoming a part of our erotic agential consent, and that can be, well, pretty pleasurable.

Just as you might allow a trusted lover to blindfold you, you can choose to trust that, while you can't see where these constricting seasons are leading you, you can be touched and touch without seeing. You can make love and be made love to in the unknowing. What is tying you up, what is constraining you, can become part of a creative erotic movement of *making* when you say yes to it. When you choose it back.

After I had weaned Rowan, I went on a retreat in the Sonoran Desert led by Cynthia Bourgeault on desert spirituality and the Desert Fathers and Mothers. We had been studying the writings of these pioneers of Christian mysticism and monasticism, who in the third century felt the growing incompatibility between the essence of Christian teaching and the institutionalization of Christianity taking place in the empire (a quandary many

Christians might currently relate to). So they up and left. Literally left their homes in the city and, one by one, began setting up camps in caves and small abodes in the desert . . . where, in solitude and closer proximity to the environment, they could proceed to live out their spiritual practices and values in peace.

"I want you to go out into the desert and pick a spot," we were told. "Draw a five-to-six-foot circle around yourself in the ground and sit there for four hours. No food, no journal, no book, no phone, no 'spiritual plan for enlightenment.' Just water, you, and a hat. And see what happens." I was still stuck on the "no book or journal" part of the instructions as everyone began dispersing into the desert landscape.

We had just been exploring one of the sayings: "Sit in your cell, and it will teach you everything." I mean, for a thirty-one-year-old starved to plumb the depths of mystical writings and desperate to experience the heights of consciousness and transcendence, this saying wasn't exactly blowing back my mystical hair. But Cynthia had simply offered a very preliminary observation on the energetic power of constraints before promptly kicking us out into the desert for this experiment.

Determined to be the ever-perfect student, I bounded out into the wilderness and proceeded to boulder up to the highest cliff perch I could manage on the side of a mountain. This still makes me giggle. How precious that I simply had to find the best view for my six-foot circle cell.

Once properly established, the sitting began. And it didn't take more than an hour before I started to feel the slow creep of anxiety and resistance. My mind began doing Cirque du Soleil somersaults and flips, and my every instinct was to simply resort to daydreaming and fantasy . . . or a nap. But I remembered that it was a choice. That I had chosen to come. That I was choosing to be here and that I wanted this. And this simple practice of (re)membering my intention began to slowly still me . . . and as I stilled, the miraculous happened. As I became more and more present, I became more and more *membered* to what was around me. Every little leaf that moved on every dry bush, the small sighing sounds of little insects, the quiet sovereignty of the tall cacti, the occasional caw of a crow in the distance. And it wasn't just the life that was evident; it was the life that doesn't often get noticed. The warmth of the rock on the face of the mountain and its quiet solidity and maternal-like embrace. I was aware of the air as it moved, and because of it, I was nourished by it.

In the constraint of the experiment, my perception tuned to a more receptive frequency, and the more present I became . . . the more enlivened and relating-and-related-to I felt. The rest of the hours passed quickly. I wasn't blissed out in some mystical enlightenment. I was simply present in my body and in that place. And via presence, I was fed by and communing with something far subtler and far more vital than our usual modes of operation.

Sit in your cell, and it will teach you everything.

Your constraints, whatever they may be, can become alchemized by the power of your choice into a womb of transformation and creativity.

Limitations force and create a container . . . whether those limitations are time, money, resources, circumstances, or seasons. The edges of everything we think is "holding us back" from what we want, or wish for, can become the boundaries that actually hold something new and unimagined in the midst of everything we think isn't "right." The only spell that is needed for this magical shift is *your conscious choice.*

My life completely turned upside down when I had kids, yes . . . absolutely. But I chose my constraints back. And precisely because I didn't have all the time in the world to fuck around on my guitar and mess with mic presets, I was able to bust out killer vocal single-takes in little ten-minute spurts that wound up being in campaigns for Victoria Secret, Trojan, and *Orange Is the New Black.* And because I was (re)membered to being more than a human-life-sustainer and milk-producer, I could choose the constraints of those precious days with a tiny toddler and newborn . . . and really, really be present to the hilarity, ecstasy, and agony of it all.

When the Victoria Secret ad ran in the middle of the VS runway Christmas show, I sat there reveling that I, a totally exhausted milk-stains-on-every-shirt-I-owned young mom from West Michigan, had sung the sultry vocals that these giraffe-legged-alien-like-beautiful-women were prancing and swaying their nonexistent hips to practically naked. That is some deeply paradoxical nondual shit right there.

Here's the takeaway: you can sit there in whatever unchosen circumstances comprise the winter of your discontent and become passive in a pity-party made for one, or you can become (re)membered to your agency by consciously accepting your constraints as the walls of your womb. You can choose it—whatever comprises the "it"—back . . . and in the choice-making, convert the constraint into a container, into a creative womb. I dare you. Watch what happens when you do.

Chapter Eleven

The Pleasurable Choice
From Discipline to Devotion

In the arts, as in life, everything is possible provided it is based on love.

—Marc Chagall

We sat in a circle in the tiny room that served as a church on Sunday evenings in downtown Barajas, Madrid. My best friend, Jessi, and I held our classical guitars awkwardly along with the other students as we tried to will our left hands to mimic the shape Santi—our patient twenty-something-year-old guitar teacher—had just taught us. We had already learned how to do an A (not too hard), Em (even easier), G (less easy), and were now working on the D (how the fuck do I get my fingers on three different strings on two different frets so close together?!!!??). My fingers ached on the sensitive tips where I was working hard to press the strings hard enough for the sound to come out clearly. My hands felt like awkward baby giraffes, only my fingers were the legs, and I couldn't make the shapes I was supposed to quickly enough for any chord to stand. Sometimes I had to literally use my right hand to move my left fingers where I wanted them to go. *Why is this so hard????*

I looked over at Jessi, and, like with most things, she was so much more patient and graceful and *good*. I felt the heat of my frustration rising in me as it met a more pressing sense of urgency and awareness: this was my last summer in Spain. My last summer home. My last summer with my best friend.

This is dumb. Why am I even wasting my time with this?

Just then Jessi looked up at me and smiled. I returned her smile immediately. In our shared gaze were thousands of memories, admissions whispered about our dreams during sleepovers, countless occasions of conspiratorial laughter in the back row during church, promises solemnly made about the lives we wanted one day, secrets kept about boys, and unwavering belief in one another. Whereas I was all fire and intensity, entirely too outspoken and headstrong, Jessi was pure grace and beauty, as soothing as water, someone who saw the best in me and in everyone, always.

Her smile turned into a funny grimace as she tried to switch into a new chord, and we both dissolved into laughter.

"This is so hard!" she huffed as she laughed.

"Why are we here?!!!" I whispered, my whole body shaking as we let our frustration turn into silly hysteria.

"*Venga*, come on," she said in that encouraging, calm way of hers, "our parents paid for the lesson, so we might as well try."

And try we did. By the end of the summer, I still really couldn't transition smoothly from one chord to the next. But I didn't care . . . I was next to my best friend, and I soaked up every minute I could with her. It didn't matter if we were at the pool, at her vacation home in Tarragona, or back in another agonizing guitar lesson.

When the lessons were done, the summer almost over, I put my dad's classical guitar away. I didn't have a reason yet *to want to play*. And in some ways, it was easier for me to close the lid and latch away everything that was going to remind me of Spain, of home, of my best friend, and the life and dreams

I was torn away from. It was easier to try to box up and hide everything that might further shatter my already broken heart.

It wasn't until three years later in the United States, when I found out we were going to move again, that I felt my heartbreak turn into longing, felt my anger activate a deeper desire. It was as if the wound of moving again opened the floodgates for me to finally feel and express all the pent-up anguish of having left Spain. All the devastating displacement and culture shock and pain of not belonging in either the Spanish country I called home or the American one I was born in and was now living in. The torrent unleashed, I opened that guitar case and wrote my first song on that same old classical guitar, with those four to five awkward chords I had learned next to Jessi.

It was that same yearning to translate my heartbreak into music that led me to write another song and then another. I no longer thought about "practicing the guitar." The guitar became the vessel for my own healing, for my own aliveness, for my soul.

I learned a couple more chords and then found my own way to a few more, just by ear. I never learned the theory behind what I was doing. I never had a map. I didn't need one. My heart blazed its own way.

Once my motivation was driven by the fire of my desire, of my heart's yearning, learning to play the guitar wasn't a "*have to*" but a "*get to.*" I looked forward to coming home from school all day to lock myself up in my room and work on my songs. My music became my safe haven, my solace, my own magical world that kept me alive, kept me feeling, kept me going.

At the time, I wasn't conscious of what had shifted in me; I was too enthralled with this new discovery to care. But now, looking back, I can see how this unfolding event demonstrated what happens when we fuel our motivation—to learn, practice, or work on something—from desire rather than obligation.

When we transform discipline to devotion.

Discipline is the first thing we think of when it comes to trying to change . . . whether it be in developing a new habit, learning a new skill, or simply being committed to our craft or work. "I need to be disciplined about this," so you set up a new schedule, set your alarm, and *try to will yourself* to "just do it."

Maybe you read the *Artist's Way* and were determined to get up in the morning and do your morning pages. You listened to Rick Rubin's *The Creative Act* and set up a canvas and paints the next day. You came back from the retreat and committed yourself to try to really meditate every day. You went to the art supply store to get everything you needed to start sketching and even created a little art corner for yourself.

Maybe for a few days or weeks you were cruising. But then *BAM* . . . something blocked your flow: a voice crept in that made you doubt yourself, perhaps a family member or partner's needs hijacked you, or you simply woke up NOT wanting to do "the thing" you said you wanted to do. Or it's possible that "the thing" just sat there untouched . . . cushion, easel, guitar, or unfinished house project. And the longer you went without starting, the louder "its" commentary on you: "See?" some voice says as you walk past "the thing" AGAIN. "You're not an artist" or "You're a lazy, piece of . . . good for nothing . . . failure."

The mysteries of what blocks our creative discipline and our discipline in general have been written about by sages and self-help gurus, by bestselling authors and spiritual masters. Tools and catchphrases abound on the four, three, six, ten things you need to just do to unlock your productivity. Chances are you are reading this book because you are also searching for that key, the magic formula, the secret sauce that's going to turn you into *an erotically enlivened creative machine.*

I have good news and bad news for you.

Bad news first? Okay.

There is no such thing as an erotically enlivened creative machine. That's an oxymoron. But I use it to demonstrate how our culture tends to think about creativity: mainly, in terms of *productivity and quantifiable results.* We have been taught to think of ourselves, our creativity, and our relationships as *machines.* If I just punch in this sequence, I'll get this result. If I program myself to make from 9:00 a.m. to 5:00 p.m., I'll be productive. If I just give them "this," then they'll do "that."

We treat ourselves and our life-force as a transactional system, as something that just needs to be whipped into shape, controlled . . . *dominated.*

Sound familiar?

The good news? The good news is that as we bring some of those dominant forces into our awareness (the power of naming), that domination (machine) energy becomes an entity that is separate from us: we begin to discern ITs voice from ours, ITs motivation from our creative desire, ITs aggression and orientation to quantifiable results as equating success.

Just as we discovered at the start of this book, two key factors that play into erotic pleasure are context and embodiment. Likewise, understanding the context of how we've been trained to think of our creativity as a machine helps us shift into a *new* context . . . one that allows us to be embodied, present, and feel a new pleasurable possibility. Once we can recognize the systemic influences, *then* we can reframe what we mean by "work," "discipline," and "productivity" for ourselves in our daily habits and routines.

As you practice this awareness, you will begin to understand that what is needed to truly unlock your creative potential isn't just a morning-pages routine and a self-help book by your bedside but an entire spiritual and cultural liberation and revolution in how you understand yourself and your purpose.

To imagine what could be, we must learn how to unknow what has been. And the more you learn to trust the open-endedness of unknowing as *creative potentiality* rather than something to be resisted, the more you discover the capacity to create abundantly, to show up in regular cultivation of your potential out of a ravenous love: a love-force larger than all the "should," "could," "would" voices that IT (and your internalized "it") tries to drown you in. This love-force understands that your creativity is fecund and wild, and that in the rhythm of making, you sometimes have to drop some tools and pick up others . . . and none of that is a reflection of your "discipline" but rather *a signet of your devotion.*

We are makers not machines. And your capacity and desire to begin that project, finish writing that chapter, work on that habit/painting/routine are often hijacked and coerced by the bizarre but unbelievably pervasive idea that *you should be a machine.* We live in a machine-worshipping world that has tried to order and control and subdue anything that doesn't fit in ITs clock-punching workday and workweek, cog-wheel subjugating reality.

Even better news. I'm going to let you in on a dangerous secret: There is nothing wrong with you. There is nothing wrong with your creativity and how it is expressed in your life. You will never *ever* run out of creativity; it is not a "broken" thing you need to fix. Does it go through cycles of rest (like all living things)? Yes. Do you need to cultivate and respect the rhythms of creative life-force with reverence? Yes. But your creativity is not a limited quantifiable resource that you will exhaust, need to hoard, improve, or buy more of. Your creativity is also not a race or arrival point to compete or compare with others. Your creativity does not need a gatekeeper . . . no guru, no god, no pontiff, no spiritual master stands in the way of you and your connection to your creativity's abundant and joyful Source.

This secret is dangerous because we live in a world that would have you believe otherwise. To (re)member and recover this knowledge deep in your body is to declare yourself free from the systems (cultural, governmental, religious) that want to pacify you into creative dependence. To remember this knowledge is to (re)member the wild ways that have been nearly erased from our collective memory, and in becoming-membered-to this wild wisdom once more . . . we are uttering the secrets, songs, and moving in and with the rhythms of the earth's seductive collaboration in co-creating new life and life more abundant.

When I say the words *discipline in your work*, do you immediately hear a whip crack? Does your body bow? Do you feel a weight on your back?

For most of us, it is nearly impossible to not associate discipline with some version of dominance-over or control-over in the effort of being a productive (ergo, worthy) member of working society. Why? Because we live in a time when these things have become synonymous and are valued and praised in society.

Hard work has always been essential to survival, but to get to the root of how and why we've lost our life-giving joy in making, we need to hunt for the historical introduction of machinery. Now, I love technology, and I'm *not at all* saying machines are bad. You will not hear me romanticizing a time before phone GPS or washing machines. Nope, you will not.

As agricultural revolutions occurred and completely transformed how societies functioned, certain social rifts occurred among the wealthy or oppressing class (who did not have to work the fields), the laborers (who toiled incessantly, often in poverty in the fields), and the machinery that caused quick profit and increased those gaps.

Later, of course, this pattern continued in the creation of factories and, even later still, mass production. There, in that shift, we began to (understandably) view not working as "the good life" and working as "not good life," and the realm of scarcity took on new proportions in the competitive, comparison, and cutthroat greed that the Industrial Revolution gave birth to.

Along the way, the arts became a commodified bonus tack-on in society. Very few have been able to sustain a living from their art, and art-as-life-path continues to be deprioritized in schools, communities, and society, while simultaneously and paradoxically culture is fame-worshipping and entertainment-oriented. We worship at the temple of money, the new gods and goddesses who magically made it to the other side of the have and have-not divide.

As a result, we have a predominant worldview that says things like "reach for the stars," "work really hard, and you can achieve anything you want," "I work hard so I can play hard," lines that have ensconced themselves across most of the globe in workaholic rhythms where we "work" from nine to five and "live" for our nights, weekends, and vacations.

We punch in and punch out. We get costly degrees so we can work high-paying jobs to pay off the decades of debt of said degrees. We work for "the man" so that we can experience "the good life."

The good life, where we can work less because we make more money . . . right?

Because money will get us the nice house, and the nice stuff, and the nice life . . . right?

Because once we have that money, all our problems will be solved, and we live happily ever after . . . right?

Productivity *is* our Purpose . . . right???

If that were true, we wouldn't be witnessing the extremes of consumeristic society gone wrong in our ecological crisis and socioeconomic disparity. We are serving a system built on the premise of scarcity . . . that no amount of money is enough; you are in this life alone, so you better fight for / earn your place, and you are not—and never, ever will be—good/rich/pretty/talented enough.

"Not enough! Not enough!" echoes every cultural message coming in loud and clear through social media comparisons, advertisements, social normative assumptions, and religion. Every domination paradigm of power-over runs on the fuel of successfully disseminating and indoctrinating the lie of "never-enough" to the masses. Gonna go ahead and say that again so you can take that in (and go ahead and include unhealthy religion as you do):

> *Every domination paradigm of power-over runs on the fuel of successfully disseminating and indoctrinating the lie of "never-enough" to the masses.*

We are swimming in "never enough" waters that equate our worth with how much money we make, which in our time has become synonymous with our definitions of "productivity." Why? Because if we do, we will forever be blindly indentured in a system that will give us money while stripping away our life / agency / inner freedom, even as it tricks us into believing we are actually living the good life.

Even if you LOVE what you do for work and feel completely in integrity with your vocation, you likely struggle with internal narratives that self-attack when you aren't being "productive," and feel shame if you haven't gotten a lot "done," or carry a sense of conditionality about your value and worth.

Is it any wonder that we struggle with discipline? Even when we want to change habits, start a project, finish the tasks we set out, much of what blocks us remains hidden in the unconscious, mainly that we've equated discipline with needing to have power-over. Our bodies try to communicate the dissonance through exhaustion, stress, and difficulty sleeping . . . but rather than listen, we push on anyway. Only when things get really chronic do we pay attention, but even then, we tend to treat the symptoms, not the fundamental problem.

We are not machines. When your discipline is fueled by the energy of power-over, you are only perpetuating the domination paradigm that will leave you feeling dominated, enslaved to your work, and feeling that nothing you do, earn, or achieve is "enough." So if you want to stop feeling that way, you have to first stop treating your body and your creativity as a machine.

Freedom is found in the recovery of our fleshy, human, autonomous, creative agency to make . . . to be makers, to be those who are creating out of the joy and pleasure and liberation of their own creativity. Those who implicitly understand that the process is the product. And when the process feels pleasurable, playful, imaginative . . . the product will be too. To be a maker is revolutionary because it shifts us from dependency as consumers to wild wielders of power and possibility as creators . . . offering and receiving the gift of enlivenment. Of life animating more life.

So once we shift the context from one of domination (I am a machine) to one of creativity (I am a maker), what becomes our motivation to . . . well, *get shit done?* If I'm not cracking the whip of self-attack on myself, will I ever be able to make the changes I want to make, develop the habits, grow as a person and as a maker?

Yes. You can and will. The key is in shifting from thinking about productivity as an *end result* to feeling enlivened pleasure as you playfully enact the possibilities *now.* Just as I discovered a greater motivation to learn how to play the guitar through my desire to write songs, all of us can tap into Eros to find a deeper desire to catalyze the change we seek. When we transform our discipline into devotion, we are not trying to control our desire . . . but rather we are animating *an even deeper desire*, one that can truly enliven us and motivate the desire to create more, love more, gift more life.

In other words, the problem isn't your desire . . . the problem is that you're not letting yourself desire *more.*

Many of us were taught as children to internalize messages to subdue, control, and silence the "whim" of desire, essentially training that shut down a vital part of ourselves. And if you happened to grow up in a conservative Christian household or have a restrictive religious upbringing, chances are you were indoctrinated with an added apprehension toward desire, creating a confluence between desire and "worldliness," or "evil," or temptation.

Desire is not a personal devil perched on your shoulder. Desire is simply life-force fuel as it animates longing . . . which is to say it is impersonal creative energy. How you employ that creative energy is another thing, but the energy itself is amoral. Desire is the yearning that pulls you into motion, sets your sights on possibility, activates you into action. The more you cast desire as "bad" or as a "devil" that distracts you, the more you will be torn in two (which, ironically, is the meaning of devil: from diabolos, meaning "the divider"). Desire isn't the devil; *we* are because we're acting from incongruity when we create division: we disembody ourselves and elevate the mind as supreme above the body.

The problem isn't your desire; it's rather how *you* are relating and listening (or not) to your desire. If you are regularly suppressing, ignoring, or seeking to control your desire, guess what? It's gonna go on strike. And if you ignore the strike? Shit will begin going sideways.

Your body will remind you that matter *is* energy, and your body will shut down and create a forced stop. And I'm not just talking about coming down with a cold. I'm saying: your practice of disconnection and disembodiment will result in actions of true self-abandonment that harm you, others, and your ecosystem. You'll break agreements. Hurt relationships. That spiral of shame will send you in a tailspin of more damage and harm . . . all of which will create real consequences.

Approaching yourself and your body as a lover is the first step to heal that disconnection with your desire. Instead of power-over, we heal the connection with our own bodies in a reverential, loving power-with. Learning how to approach *all of our lives* from devotion instead of discipline is found in this first act of softly coming back to the body. Letting the rest of you come back online. Feeling enlivened through sensation in the present moment. Learning to listen to the body's cues and trusting it as wisdom.

Once we have shifted into a tender arousal of our full embodied presence, then (as is true of any relationship) we must begin by simply listening from a stance of curiosity, not critique. What is going on here? What is my desire trying to tell me? As we listen, we begin to learn, understand, and therefore heal into a wholeness that is creatively abundant and actively participating in hopeful making.

Desire is simply another word for Eros, for life-force. In choosing to listen, we discover that our life-force might be coopted by incongruous actions we are taking. We discover that we are not being honest with ourselves or others about agreements, or we may discover that we may be out of balance in our rhythm and simply need more rest or the quiet of solitude. We locate the internalized lies of "never enough" and "too much" that have led to unhealthy habits, behaviors, and relationships. As we listen to our desire like lovers, we are able to seduce a deeper motivation for the changes we seek to make. We are able to locate the more within that can lead to the more in our making. This will not result in a lack of creativity, manifestation, or productivity. As we listen, learn, understand, and heal our relationship with our own desire, what was once the power over "discipline" of productivity and "getting shit done" will transform like a phoenix in the ashes into something far more revolutionary, powerful, resilient, and creatively generative: *devotion*. And because devotion is fueled by love, you won't ever run out of energy or desire to keep trying, to keep expressing, to keep going.

We've all experienced the difference when a lover does something from the pure desire that comes from devotion versus duty or obligation. It's the difference between a handwritten note from the heart and store-bought flowers carelessly tossed onto the kitchen table with a "Happy anniversary. See? I remembered." Or the difference between engaging in tender, passionate, delicious seduction or saying to your partner with an eye roll, "Okay, sure. Let's have sex, but can we make it quick?" and then staring up at the ceiling, distracted and disembodied, during sex like the opening scene of *Amelie*.

Our creativity is the same way. When we show up to our work from a place of obligation, from "I have to get this done," that doesn't exactly animate or encourage erotic energy. Remember: the process is the product. So if you want the product to be good, the *process has to be good.*

Like you would with a lover, you must slow way down . . . become completely present to sensation, present in your body. Arouse your senses and tune into yourself and what you're doing until that brush stroke on the canvas is a turn on. Until the unhurried melody works itself through you with pleasure. Until the sentence sighs and sings. Tap into the desire that's deeper than "completion." The desire that has no concern with outcomes or destinations. The desire that experiences the coursing, throbbing, pulsing energy of life in every moment and recognizes it for the gift it is.

Then, and only then, does your "I have to" shift to the unhurried, gratitude-filled devotion of "I get to." And making from that place . . .

Well, it feels pretty damn good. So good, in fact, that you'll keep making.

Chapter Twelve

New Positions

Stretching with Flexible Possibility

> *Poetry and painting are done in the same way you make love; it's an exchange of blood, a total embrace—without caution, without any thought of protecting yourself.*
>
> —Joan Miró

I sat with my back up against the mirrored walls, hands gripping the wooden bar above, awaiting my torture. Olga, our ballet teacher, came and sat in front of me and placed her heels on my ankles as she pushed my legs open until the outside of my feet and ankles were perfectly aligned against the wall in a perfect 180-degree line as strings of Spanish expletives unleashed themselves in my mind. The other girls watched, lazily stretching on their own.

"Breathe," she said, bored.

I exhaled loudly through my lips and gripped the bar harder. We did this every day, this stretching torture. And the feeling of it was anguish, one your body can barely bear, making you want to erupt in tears, laughter, and a scream all at once.

Sure, we were dancers. And yeah, we were flexible AF. However, there was always the way your muscles would tense up and tighten after yesterday's work that would require the practice of stretching. And some of us were still not quite *perfect* in our splits, so we needed a little help. By "some of us," I mean . . . just me. I can still recall the sensation of that . . . of being split totally open and pinned to the wall. Of feeling like I couldn't bear it, of wanting to scream and laugh hysterically. The tension of it.

And yet, for dancers, without flexibility, there would be no movement. Strength is just one half of the lovemaking motions of ballet. Flexibility is the other. What emerges from the mingling of both is the grace of the choreography, of the dance itself.

But, *sweet Jesus*, it hurts like hell to be pushed and stretched like that. Mere minutes felt like years. We cannot make, change, be transformed, or integrate a damn thing without the body. Embodiment is the only way we create, love, grow. It's how we are grounded in the physical and the natural world . . . because they remind us that nothing, nothing happens apart from the body.

Early conception, for instance, is marked by the sudden onset of disruptive and uncomfortable symptoms. It is the gradual dawning of the realization that your life is not "yours" anymore. But one of the facets of these pregnancy changes is centering around the body's need to shift, adjust, and stretch to make room for the new life that has taken hold within. Later on, in the pregnancy, the stretching is quite literal: your rib cage literally shifts and opens like a butterfly to allow your heart to almost entirely flip, all while abdominal muscles stretch and pull apart to make room for the organs to be squished up, while the uterus grows five hundred times bigger than its original size to house the growing baby.

Shifting, opening, and making room. The starting line of conception is rife with a tsunami of hormones that soften ligaments, the creation of gland pathways, and changes that stretch the body.

With every stage of this erotic invitation, you are invited into the increasing awareness of being comfortable with discomfort as essential to creativity. "Creativity takes courage," said Matisse. Why? Because it requires embodied vessels that are grounded, stable, relaxed, brave. You think that new ideas just *appear*? New paintings just *happen*? New songs just roll in . . . just like *that*? Only when we've finally learned how to relax (not panic or grasp), soften and yield (not harden against), surrender (not resist), trust (not fear) can we be ready to open to the ultimate loss of control when the womb becomes fertile with new possibility.

Every new life, project, idea, vision, relational stage goes through a new conception phase. And rarely is it pretty. It's messy . . . and you might feel like you've been hijacked by a tiny alien (my personal experience of early conception). You will be uncomfortable. But what else would nature use as a two-by-four to the head to make the necessary life adjustments to nurture that tiny, fledgling new possibility into a miraculous manifestation?

Stretching is never a comfortable experience . . . especially when it feels like it's being done to you. Just like the agonizing stretching in ballet that Olga used to put us through, it is *almost unbearable.*

Creative life, though, asks us to stretch in every phase of early conception. In the gradual apprehension of a new idea, vision, possibility—when what once worked suddenly doesn't—we experience the discomfort that develops the flexibility needed to make room for the new to emerge in and through us. The way creativity works, there's a counterintuitive call to relax into our natural discomfort in the midst of the changes as we stretch and switch tools, instruments, and mediums.

When we soften into willingness, power-with (not the egoic and controlling power-over), and we don't seize up, constrict, or fight against what is emerging . . . new life will come. If we stretch *with* new life so that it has a chance of being born through us.

The lessons of stretching are simple: *relax*, lean in, yield, and breathe into those tight spaces. Relax your instinct to tense up, armor up, stay hidden, or protected. Stay with the ache that makes. In our creative lives that looks like learning how to be nimble, imaginative, and nonidentified as we make room for these new ideas to grow . . . as we move toward the tender places in ourselves. Stretching calls for Eros—so switch positions . . . and be playful about it.

In sex, we know that trying out new positions is part of what leads to discovering new levels of pleasure and intimacy. And sure, at first it might be awkward, and it's impossible not to dissolve into laughter somewhere along the journey if you're aiming to exhaust the options. But the willingness to stretch and try new things is part of erotic enlivenment . . . part of creativity.

Coming home from that fateful trip on which I was assaulted, with so much tender in me, I sat down at our old piano and played. What came out of me was nothing short of laughable. I—the queen of low, throaty, crooning, guitar-driven indie folk—suddenly was writing high, breathy, pop R&B on the piano. Mind you, I didn't play the piano . . . or at least I didn't until then. I thought it was ridiculous and clearly just a weird rando creative hiccup.

As a joke, I sent three of these demos over to a producer friend, Daniel, with the text "I am having a pop hairball. Please stand by while I hack it up."

Much to my surprise, Daniel didn't think it was laughable at all. He loved the demos and asked me to keep sending them his way. Within two weeks, I had written every single song that would eventually be released on the *Feminine Tense* record we put out together two years later under the collaborative duo Avila.

Now when I look back, it makes sense that after the trauma I experienced, my body needed to create music it could move to . . . with driving beats that reminded me of that day when Little Dragon's rhythmic songs helped me walk myself back to freedom in Amsterdam by urging me onward to the Stedelijk Museum.

My body needed to dance its way out of the violence of what had happened and be (re)membered to my own sovereignty, agency, and eternal fluidity. And my voice needed to get high, breathy, and move in a whole different register to express how utterly vulnerable we are as women in this masculine-ruled world where things like this still happen every day. Everywhere.

That album will always be one of my proudest creative accomplishments, and believe me, it has nothing to do with sales or recognition. I am proud because of how much healing those songs created in me through an entirely new register and genre. I had to stretch way . . . WAY . . . out of my comfort zone as a musician and singer to make room for what was wanting to come through me in *Feminine Tense.* Sometimes being willing to sing in a different way to discover the sound of our true voice calls us into a wild and new creative expression.

When the DC organization that I worked for went belly up and I was wandering in the wastelands of "oh shit, now what?" it was not writing music that called to me at first . . . but a totally different medium. It was the quiet and steady work of painting that I craved and seemed to soothe the panic in me. For months, I returned to one single canvas and rode the nauseating waves of unknowing through my devotion to simply show up before my painting and offer it a little more of myself each day.

As I painted, I channeled my restlessness into a work of art that made room for me to carry the question of "what will I do next?" long enough for it to turn into the pregnancy of the *Unknowing* podcast, a new album, and a vision of centering all those expressions. As the image revealed itself before me on my canvas, a new image of myself began to form itself within me.

Sometimes being willing to switch tools, instruments, and mediums creates space for a new vision to emerge in our hearts and lives. Sometimes we need to spice things up and switch positions with our partner and get playful to conceive a new level of desire in the relationship. Sometimes we need to stretch and be stretched. The process is usually one that isn't comfortable at first . . . like having your feet pinned to the wall by Olga or finding out you're pregnant. You might find yourself screaming some colorful language (go ahead!). But you can trust the process.

New life will always make us uncomfortable. Will always switch things up, will always stretch us. This is how frustration breeds creativity.

A road map of stretch marks runs across my stomach for the two Viking-sized babies I carried in my small five-feet, four-inch frame. So, believe me, I know that stretching is never easy. It is scary, uncomfortable, awkward, and strange. Underneath all the weird, though, is the wild wonderful of new life. New possibility. Moreness.

Go ahead, try a new position. Switch tools. Grab that bar. Take a deep breath and let life pin you to the wall. Stretch it, baby. All this discomfort is going to make you one hell of a dancer.

Chapter Thirteen

More than Words
No Explanation Required

> *I found I could say things with color and shapes that I couldn't say any other way—things I had no words for."*
>
> —Georgia O'Keeffe

I was walking with a friend through a particularly beautiful and preserved piece of land in Michigan . . . full of the natural beauty of tall grasses and trees and a river. The sun was hanging low in the sky the way it does here in the summer, and everything was gilded in gold. Overhead an eagle called out and was quickly joined by another. Too mired in my own emotions, I was only half-present to the beauty around me.

"I just feel all jumbled inside. I know I should be grateful for this job, but I feel this longing . . . a longing that makes no sense. I want to just make music, and write, and be an artist. But how do I square that with reality? Is that just some part of me that doesn't want to grow up?"

My friend Mandy looked at me sideways. "Is that what you think about your art? That it's an immaturity?"

"No, I mean . . . it's just that with all things that are too good to be true, I feel I need to justify it. Like it doesn't add up with the realm of 'responsible adulthood' with the retirement plan and rainy-day fund."

She got very quiet. And then she asked, "Do you justify love?"

"No."

"Then why do you feel you need to justify this part of yourself? Does love require risk?"

"Yes, of course."

"This is no different. Brie, for as long as I've known you, you can't help but create . . . make music, or write, or express what is in you in an artistic way. But for as long as I've known you, you've also felt the need to apologize for who you are, make yourself smaller or less . . . to fit in or belong. You are shrugging while minimizing yourself and thinking that it's what is expected. But what if you didn't have to explain it or yourself anymore? Not just to others," she added quietly, "but to yourself?"

I stopped midstep. Letting her words sink in.

Like the liquid gold of the setting sun, wonder spread through me. Suddenly the thrumming life all around me seemed to be singing this same unapologetic song . . . from the eagles overhead, to the trees shimmering with amber light, to the river rushing nearby: nature does not require an explanatory preamble to its existence. So why would I? *What if I didn't have to justify who I was? What if I didn't have to explain it anymore . . . to anyone or to myself?*

It was one of the many mic-drop moments I've experienced with my friend Mandy over the years. Looking back on it now, it's so clear . . . I was already beginning to clarify where my longing was leading me as the world—and the organization I was working for—came to a hard stop during the pandemic. And in these years that followed, Mandy's question has stayed with me like a mantra.

What if I didn't have to explain myself anymore?

As creatives, we often get stuck in the cycle of explanation and justification. We feel that if we can paint a cohesive picture in our minds and for others about what the perfect finished product or piece is, then and only then can we begin making it. While claiming we are willing to risk big, the truth is we're saying to ourselves and others, "Okay, I'll risk big once my insurance policy is updated . . . and once I hedge my bet these six different ways . . . and once I consult and run my idea by every mentor I have and their mother and their mother's neighbor." But when we seek to justify the risk of stepping into the unknown with a sense of certainty . . . is that courageous creative risk a leap of faith? Or more calculated control?

Until that point, I justified my fear of stepping into my own truth as an artist by clinging to the social normative belief that being an artist is irresponsible because it's financially risky. Because you won't be able to play the capitalist consumer game of "having" and "security" as an artist. Because there are no maps that can safely predict the product when the entire process of being an artist is a devotion to unknowing. Single motherhood also carries a story of self-sacrificial duty, which rationalized resignation to my job because it provided a stable income.

No, I'm not saying you should be reckless . . . but you do have to be courageous, and sometimes being courageous seems reckless to others or to your inner critic you spend so much time justifying yourself to.

What if you didn't have to explain yourself anymore?

There is something deeply embodied and powerful about discovering your own sovereignty and agency. And it begins when you realize you no longer feel the need to explain your most courageous decisions. For me, it was the moment I noticed the sun go gold and Mandy's words turned into a mantra. As I looked to the trees around me, I drew from them the permission to stand tall in my desire, not as a selfish whim but as *what makes me me.* An inner alignment begins to form as you give yourself permission to be your truest self and believe that this selfhood is eternally bound to the larger fabric of belonging that can't be displaced by risk, failure, or any success. Only from that rooted place of your noncontingent worth and belonging (the embodied present, radical enough-ness) can you branch outward in new and surprising ways and expand to heights beyond your wildest dreams. And yes, it comes at a cost. There is always a reciprocal energetic exchange. We hand over our sense of control in moments of great risk, but the return is that we develop a capacity to trust that the unknowing will reveal a larger possibility for us than we imagined for ourselves.

What if you didn't have to explain yourself?

The truth is, no one is ever ready for love to turn our lives upside down and gift us with more beauty than we knew existed. It's sort of like asking, "How do I know if we're ready to have kids?" The truth is you never will be . . . because you literally cannot conceive or imagine the wonder of it. Which is terrifying. And absolutely the magic of it.

Here's the wild truth of all creativity: we can't fully imagine what hasn't been created . . . until we decide to create it.

Only when we stop locking up our creative energy in internal or external exhausting explanations, justifications, or risk assessments can we jump in . . . and make what we never imagined. Do what didn't seem possible. Try what seemed too risky. Creativity belongs to the brave. To those who are willing to imagine and bring forth the "what could be," not to those stuck wasting their energy on the peanut gallery of the "what is."

I'm writing this during one of the countless sleepless nights I have had since taking my own big courageous leap into the unknown. So this is not touting the magical thinking of "just manifest it, and it will all be fine." I am totally unsure of how I will make ends meet. Yet here is the truth: I may have lost financial security, but I gained myself . . . my inexhaustibly abundant erotic freedom, joy, and creativity. I am terrified but in an exhilarated way. I am squeezed at times on all sides like a birth canal, sure, but I've also never been more alive or given birth to so much life. My life is being lived now on the growing edges of its expansion into *moreness*, which provides me with daily opportunities to surrender to unknowing, (re)member, and imagine a new way. I am creating with my whole heart, soul, and *body*. I trust my instincts. I trust myself.

In an effort to follow the *en vogue* philosophical ideals that the good, perfect, and all-powerful must be unchanging, we created a seemingly irreparable rift between this material world and what we conceived as "divine." And as the enlightenment swept us in its thrall of rationality-over-all . . . we've rendered whatever was beyond the scope of the rational mind into mere superstition. As a result, we've become accustomed to assigning a sense of inferiority to our embodied instincts as nonintelligence, and as untrustworthy.

Erotic creativity is the remembered instinct. The instinct of the body's sovereign agency. By dismissing the instinctual, we cut ourselves off from our membership to embodied humanity and belonging in this deeply relational reality. To be a generative, courageous creative, to be human, you need this superpower fully activated and turned on. Without erotic creativity, you will not be here. You will not be able to discern or hear—let alone speak/sing/make in—your true, authentic voice, and you will instead feel like an echo of yourself . . . perpetually making things that sound like someone else.

When a woman is pregnant, her body's instincts go into high gear. Her cravings are an expression of nutrient needs she is deficient in, nutrients necessary to support the new life inside her.

In the early conception of our next creative contributions, we meet that same embodied need. To deny or dismiss the realm of embodied intuition means we force ourselves into a creative anemia that inevitably causes us to lean too heavily, draw from, or copy what has already existed before. It takes a tremendous amount of grounded, rooted, and embodied awareness to sort out the sound of our true voice urging us into the unknown, yet-unimagined "could be." You cannot enter in any other way.

As with the early stages of conceiving my new life as a maker with my album *Me Veo*, I became inexplicably drawn to wearing my vintage silk kimonos. I painted in the ecstatic relief of the unknown, trans-verbal. I listened to records I hadn't put on in years. I looked at old postcards when drafting lyrics. For weeks and weeks this went on.

I was feeling my way into what I wanted to create . . . something silky soft, unapologetically sensual, a feminine feline purr working itself out of me as if my soul was cat-stretching. I was seducing the muse and (re)membering myself in the process. The becoming-me was the embodiment of everything I needed to say and how I needed to say it. When the words began forming themselves in the melodies I was creating, they were in French, Spanish, and English. While I am bilingual in Spanish and English, I don't consider my high-school French to be on par with the other two. So . . . why the hell did French come in?

Simply because the songs required it. They wanted it, and the woman I was becoming was confident enough to meet the requirements of creative work. When the concepts solidified, I realized the postcards gave me permission to create stories and imagined possibilities, to deepen the true stories that were the seeds of the songs. Each image, each piece of fabric, each language, each song let my instincts take over.

Creatives become a bloodhound that has the scent of possibility. Follow the oxygen: what draws you, what sounds good, what feels right. Sniff it out, follow it, and stop questioning it. It may ask you to completely switch up your routines, your daily rituals, your traditions. It may ask you to take dancing lessons, practice a new hobby, speak in or learn a new language.

Go with it. Move with the realm of the embodied instincts asking you to trust . . . to play . . . to experiment. Let yourself trust that your cravings are there for a reason and stop dismissing them as dumb, silly, ridiculous, or irresponsible.

What if you didn't have to explain yourself anymore?

Moving beyond our rational mind's need to order, organize, and justify everything is what we do in love (and imagination, faith, eroticism). The sweet sigh of surrendered relief from the mind's perpetual prattling is what we experience in sex and prayer and hope. You dissolve into a trust that transcends "reason." No longer needing to translate yourself anymore, you simply feel, imagine, love, live, and become.

A new liquid-gold light will glow through you, in the warmth of a smile and self-assured radiance of no longer needing to justify yourself. Like a sunset that settles and lulls the questioning mind as it gives way gracefully to the unknowing night. The exhilarating freedom you will experience when you become so aligned. Like trees who have no need to defend a thesis to stand so proud, so tall. The thrill and adventure that comes by being willing to risk and fly like the birds overhead, sweeping and diving and crying out with delight for no reason at all.

Imagine everything that you can't imagine waiting for you on the other side, beyond your explanations. Beyond all words. Beauty doesn't have to explain itself. And neither do you.

Chapter Fourteen

Courageously Vulnerable

Letting In, Letting Go, and Setting Free

There's a crack in everything, that's how the light gets in.
—Leonard Cohen

The courage to walk through the fissures of our broken hearts, into the unknowing beyond, is the most genuinely brave creative act. Learning how to trust moving past the broken edges of what has been or even what we hoped into the darkness of "could be" is vital for new life and new possibility . . . we just have to learn how to not get hooked on the edges of our own heartbreaks, disappointments, or losses.

For months, I had been in a weird music limbo no-man's-land well known to every musician: negotiating a contract. The publishing company courting me to sign with them was new and attempted to be a hybrid publishing and artist services company, essentially replacing the need for a label. I was excited by the idea of growing together and the dedicated attention and representation an innovative company like this would provide. I was also daring to believe that the financial compensation the contract would provide could finally help cover the gap between what I was making and what I need to survive . . . an existential exhale started to work itself out of my lungs. Only to get the wind knocked out of me with a gut punch in the end. As a new pub company, it was still getting some of its core funding in place, and in a last-minute unforeseen shift, several investors pulled out. And—with them no longer able to staff for and sign new artists—the deal was dropped.

Few things will vampire the hope and energy of an artist more than release delays on material we've been pregnant with for so long. Several years ago, this would have tanked me. The self-pity and victim-making-villains' cultural sway would have flooded me. But something else entirely happened.

I have given a lot of thought to our ideas of "failure" and what arbitrary contours define its monstrous shape in the shadows, in the dark woods and unknowing night of "what if." We all have stories that create what goes "bump" in the night: *What if I lose my job? What if my marriage doesn't make it? What if I put myself out there and I'm ridiculed? What if my courage costs my security of belonging?*

What's fascinating is how the "what if" worst-case scenarios grow in our imaginations, becoming so powerful they scare us into freezing in place . . . spook us into hiding in our own beds of comfort and familiarity, certain that if we dare to step out, some boogie-man-of-what-might-be will get us. So . . . my pub deal fell through. Is that a failure? To many it might. It certainly was a disappointment. But disappointments are not fixed definitions. Inviting us to a different outlook on our heartbreak, poet David Whyte writes, "The measure of our courage is the measure of our willingness to embrace disappointment, to turn towards it rather than away, the understanding that every real conversation of life involves having our hearts broken somewhere along the way and that there is no sincere path we can follow where we will not be fully and immeasurably let down and brought to earth, and where what initially looks like a betrayal, eventually puts real ground under our feet."

In the great firmament dome of my sky, I see "failures" as the figures that tear open our artificial, curtained categories . . . as the piercing holes that let in the light. I see failures as fallopian horns and a vulva smile, the ultimate uterine face that can shed both the losses of un-met maybes and pleasurably receive the possibility of what could yet be.

Failure is just a fermentation of our fear. A flux that puts us in touch with the fallacy of each one of our constructs, and because of this . . . every failure is really just a composting beginning. A surrendered release of our expectations of what we thought might or should have been into a joyful undoing of our own concepts, ideas, identifications on a great hopeful heap of what we cannot yet imagine.

What does the fallacy of failure look like? What defines the lines of its monstrous face? What shadowy shapes does it take on in the dark of *your* unknown? Whether we realize it or not, we assign the determination of "failure" to pretty much anything that doesn't go the way we plan. To any no we receive instead of a yes. To every attempt at collaboration/partnership that wound up having to diverge.

But letting go of control, a circumstance, or our expectations is the creative act.

None of us is ever ready for the moment. The moment when our grip actually loosens and the other hand slips out of ours. The moment we relinquish control over outcome and become vulnerable to the world in acceptance of what is, what has been, what we've done/built/created and given. The moment when we exhale our trust in the shape of a step, a "send," a "publish," or the bittersweet taste of one final kiss goodbye. The moment we acknowledge that the love shared between us was real. And sometimes that love shapes itself into even stronger bonds, and other times that love catalyzes a closure (chosen or not), a cauterizing that takes time to accept.

Letting go is not easy.

We make plans, and they do not go the way we thought they would. We imagine an outcome, and it doesn't occur the way we hoped. We envisioned a future that did not come to pass.

To let go is to be in the flow of all of life that must constantly adjust to the reality of the "what is" moment by moment. To let go is to be in perpetual acceptance, to be willing to embrace that change is the only constant. So here is the thing:

To let go . . . is to live.

To be alive is to be willing to be in perpetual renewal . . . at a cellular, bodily, spiritual, emotional level. So it follows that if we want to be fully alive—to live a life of courage and creativity—we need to be fully ready to learn to let go again and again and again. And hopefully, as a muscle that is being developed, each time with a little more ease and grace and grit. The way to let go is to first learn how to really and truly *hold* . . . to acknowledge the gift before you give it away.

Thinking we can just jump straight into the liberation stage, many of us miss that critical step, miss doing the work of breathing through the pain of loss by choosing to focus with gratitude for what was shared . . . allowing gratitude to reorient us into a stance of erotic generosity and generativity.

It would be like a tree saying it's ready for winter without first having held leaves or allowing generosity to shade it brightly in a riot of celebrated surrender. We, too, must do that same work. To begin the work of letting go, we first hold in our hands the truth of what we've been gifted through that relationship, expression, or experience. It is the choice to pause and say, "This was a gift, this was enough . . . even though it didn't go the way I hoped, this is enough."

When things don't go the way we hoped or planned, we return to the here and now and (re)member that our worth isn't tied to outcomes. We choose to reframe what has happened as an understandable disappointment, not a definition or a failure. We choose to reframe the no as a redirection, not rejection.

We choose vulnerability; we accept it and stay soft . . . even though it's the hardest part. Because staying soft and fleshy is the way of erotic creativity, it's the way of love and life and beauty and everything that keeps us human instead of machine.

When trees drain of chlorophyll with the growing absence of the sun in the fall, the leaves reveal their true color. It's the chlorophyll that makes the leaves green. Without chlorophyll, what is revealed is the truth of the leaves all along.

As the leaves release, they form a nutrient-rich, protective layer over the root systems, allowing a nourishing cycle to continue. Deep within and below the ground, the mycorrhizal root networks are buzzing with water and nutrients and sugars that are pushed out by the largest trees for miles surrounding them. They are letting out into their network all the gifts for their shared survival, including their symbiotic relationships with the fungal networks that help form their lines of communication, their "wood wide web" that helps them send chemical, hormonal, and slow-pulsing electrical signals (warnings, information, or distress).

The letting go . . . the surrender of vulnerability when things don't go like we wanted . . . is an offering, a giving. It is part of the creative cycle's release that we see play out in the changing seasons: the surrender to life as it takes the gifts of one season and metabolizes them, composts them, digests them into a new living season ahead.

How often do we think about our losses or disappointments as *part* of the creative cycle? How often do we pause to consider how entering fully into our heartbreak and welcoming in the love and lessons learned are the two prerequisite steps for us to fully metabolize a "loss" into a "gift," one that can nourish not just our growth but also the network of relationships around us?

When we can accept that the ache is the love and absorb the growth that we have experienced because of that person/

place/circumstance, we soften and relax our nervous systems into allowing a creative metabolizing to occur. The chlorophyll of all that "doing" and "trying" relaxes and descends into our bodies, revealing the brightly colored truths that simply and boldly declare "what is" (and what has been) true all along. *That hurt. Their choices really disappointed me. That didn't go the way I hoped.* But also: *I realize. I'm becoming aware. I'm discovering.*

That profound translation and metabolization is a sacred turn that occurs when we let go, when we soften and surrender with gratitude to do what was, and in so doing, make space for a new "could be." We translate what we are learning into *a nourishing letting out.* This "letting out" is a *setting free*, not just of the other person, circumstance, or season . . . but of ourselves.

Maybe it looks something like this. You have coffee with a friend and choose to be vulnerable about the pain of your loss, the gifts of what you are learning, and, in sharing, unknowingly nourish your friend's own letting go, letting in, and letting out process.

You soften into the hurt, choose not to vilify or flatten reality into binaries, and instead move in a posture of composting trust. You choose to stay in flow as you work on a new painting, project, song, idea . . . unknowingly channeling all that autumnal digesting into something that nourishes and inspires others' creative cycling.

You quietly grieve and, in the grieving, find the gratitude for what is true, for the revelations of beauty in the midst of it all, and while you may not have words to make meaning out of what is happening within you . . . something has shifted how you interact with others and move through your day. A certain grace is hovering in and around you . . . like the rich fragrance of a surrender, a mulching into love.

What happens in these moments of our metabolizing loss, redirections, disappointment, or heartbreak is that—as you return to the (re)membering that you are not defined by these outcomes or by the little fragile egoic "me"—you become *more than you, which is your leaf-colored truth all along.*

Our disappointments, loss, and hurt can be metabolized precisely because they reacquaint us with the forested root system network that has always sustained us. And in that metabolization, we become a processing nourishing force for the "we" that has been more-than-me all along. Our metabolizing *is* our creating. Our grieving *is* our making. You don't have to rationalize it into meaning to feel the process alive in your body.

Is saying goodbye to a lover really any different than the surrender that was made when we let that lover in? Both require the courage of staying soft. Of vulnerability, of fleshy feeling. Without learning to be vulnerable, to let go and be open-handed and open-hearted, you will miss out on the chance to give love and feel loved. You lose your ability to ground in the deep abiding sense of belonging and reciprocity that makes life so wondrous, so magical, and so fulfilling. When we are grounded in that deeper trust, we can flow in the rhythms of life and love that erotically give and take, seduce and push back, receive and express, let in and let out . . . because that is *how we make love.*

Eros is enlivened as we let go of what has been, let in what could be, and let our love, hope, and magic out in everything we give.

If you want to live the life of courageous creativity, you have to learn to let go again and again. Let go of the idea of arrival, the idea that fulfillment is "out there" (instead of "already here"). Let go of believing that having or possessing is the answer to your deepest yearnings. You have to let go of the safety of knowing, of our tendency to want to control, to have assured certainties. Let go of the outcome. Let go of the identities or labels you are tempted to cling to when things don't go as you hoped.

And as you learn to let go, you will receive something far more vital: *you will be fulfilled simply by the absolute miracle of being a living part of this creative and creating world.* You will be set free.

As I write this, I have no great award to my name. No fame or accolades. And I have never been more alive, more fulfilled, more clear in my entire life. Every step I take, I discover a new way to not be intimidated, a new level of freedom in my body and being, a new wellspring of humor and humility, a new depth of love and wonder for this life and the creatures in it. I live in the joyful resonance that I have touched on everything I am offering you and felt the truth of it in my own body. I sit here with nothing, but I have everything. I am fulfilled by giving this life everything I am.

* * *

You and I began this journey like a first blush of a first date. And with every turning page, the relationship deepened into intimacy, into the pleasurable possibility of *more.* You've held my whole heart in your hands this entire time, and with each page you turned, you were willing to deepen into the love offered. The erotic surrender of every word I gave you as an offering of love became fodder and mulch for your own wild becoming. And just like all of life requires us to let go, dear reader, we, too, now part.

In every Polaroid memory given, in this disclosure of my body's field notes on becoming, is the gift of my love. My art is as intimate to me as my own blood, my own flesh . . . because it's only through my body that I have this authority. I hope you've felt me reaching out through these words, touching you. I hope you've felt my breath in the words I've spoken. I hope you've felt the warmth of my soft body as I've embraced you, as I gave every bit of myself away on each page you've read.

Can you feel me? I'm right here with you.

You don't have to create a choice, a false dichotomy between a life of creative risk or a life of safety . . . it *can* be, it *is,* both.

Only your safety will not come from external influences, validation, or attainments but your own unshakable trust in yourself . . . in your noncontingent worth. And the risks you take from that courageous place will be of greater and greater vulnerable generosity, a life of brave creativity. You enliven as you enliven others. You are found as you are given. And nothing you have ever offered—no love shared, no glance, no little melody sung, no sketch, no touch, no laughter, no tear—is ever lost or wasted in this world.

Can you feel it too? We are what we give.

When we give ourselves away in love, we have nothing to fear. There's no "away," eco-theologian Brian McLaren said to me once in a conversation, reflecting with me on the ecological principle. There is no throwing anything away. There is no apart.

The power-over fear-based rhetoric of the domination paradigm will always seek to dismember us from this relatedness of being. You, here. Me, here. Us, together in this moment, feeling our shared becoming. It will seek to cut off, cut away, and "throw away." It will declare the worthy and seek the erasure of the unworthy. It will always seek to create false narratives, identities, and categories of success and failure.

The power-with invitation of the erotic-creative life, however, is one of relating, not dominating . . . so everything is in relationship to everything else. Nothing is thrown away; nothing is wasted.

The revelation of this wonderful web-like recognition is that you have nothing to lose. Literally. Your bank account may fluctuate, but you yourself—*You*—will not "lose" anything.

There is no failure.

There is no failure.

From this moment onward, there is only growth, only learning, stretching, shifting, embodied unfolding, and deepening along the way. When everything gets composted, everything belongs . . . and every facet of this adventure is an opportunity for your creative lovemaking to become more and more authentic and beautiful.

In love and in life, we are made by what we courageously give. The quality of our conscious love is manifest in our creative outpouring . . . through every tear, sweat drop, ache of a muscle. Through each morning we get up in hope, in courage, and keep going. Through the resonance and timbre of your inimitable voice. The softness of your skin, the touch and feel of you . . . alive and connected and touching . . . earth, grass, skin, bark, air, water. Your heart pumping, your giving, taking in, holding. Your breath moving . . . in and out . . . like your love, animating your erotic core as you choose what to make of your life.

So my parting request to you, love, is this: Turn yourself *on*. Be willing to discover your embodied presence as the key to letting more matter than your mind . . . as the key to your wildest and most authentic creativity. As the key to helping you let go of what you think you know to make room for what could be.

Be willing to awaken to Eros, the creative life-force in and all around you. Eros is always here, so, really, *be here*. And by that presence, be willing to play . . . create . . . make. Let yourself become erotically enlivened by a longing that cannot help but pour itself out of you and into this world, to shatter your own heart open like a precious jar and let the fragrance of you fill every space.

Find who you really are . . . by giving yourself away fully as a gift to this world and in every possible way.

Create, love . . . and so, *become*.

Acknowledgments

As I've written in the pages of this book, creativity is communal . . . and I couldn't have created this work without the threads of a web that sustain me, support me, and gift me the opportunity to give myself away in art and love every day. The anchors to this web are my family: my parents, David and Wendy Stoner; my boys, Søren and Rowan; and their amazing father, Steve Mayer. My brother, Santino Stoner, and my sister-in-law, Francesca.

To my parents: you have gifted me with an embodiment of what love looks like through my whole life but especially as you've stood by me in the last several years, continually offering me literal and emotional support. Your belief has been the buoyancy that has kept me afloat through the hardships of choosing this life of being a maker, with your constant encouragement, your availability, your help with the kids, the love offered over countless meals, conversations, and hidden within dropped-off bags of groceries. Mom, you are my original creative icon . . . the woman who has taught me how to believe in what is possible, to pick up a pen and write a new ending. I hope you feel yourself reflected in the tenacity you have instilled in me through the countless moves, courageous willingness to step into the adventure of the unknown, and the capacity to cast a spell in the lines and shapes of words that can inspire others. Thank you. Santino, thank you for being part of my soul's blueprint, my co-creative conspirator of moreness in this life, for walking beside me through thick and thin, and for the courage you have lent me on countless occasions when mine was dwindling. Thank you for bravely showing me what coloring outside the lines looks. Fran, your love, loyalty, humor, tenacity, and strength has become so much a part of our family's weft and weave that I can't imagine an "us" without you. Thank you for your encouragement and love.

To my Creatures: my wild, wonderful boys . . . you are my teachers, and I am continually inspired by your magic, your wonder, your kindness. Thank you for the gift of being witness to your own unfolding and for the grace with which you navigate living in more than one world. Thank you for eating breakfasts around plaster and paint, for sharing me with the studio when I'm recording, and for knowing that even when I'm on the road, the spiderweb that connects our hearts is forever intact. I am in awe of who you are becoming, and it is my greatest joy in life to watch you create your own story. Steve, you are the greatest co-parent any mother could wish for . . . thank you for your kind devotion and unwavering, steadfast presence as a father and co-parent. Your friendship after all the heartbreak we have endured is a gift I do not take for granted.

My web is also comprised of women who form a coven around me. Kathryn York, you have believed in this creative hurricane from the first day we met in Silver Lake as couple of twentysomething babies. We've been sisters in every lifetime, I'm sure of it. Lindsay Branham, thank you for the years of voice memos and the courage of love notes offered and shared as we continue to stand to our own feet "in the midst of the cosmos." Joy Williams, Kimbra Johnson, and Angie Mattson, each of you has inspired me as creatives and fanned the ember in my own heart into a roaring flame. Felicia Murrell, my stealing-shrimp-via-purses-from-cocktail-parties soul sister, thank you for calling this book forth out of me years ago. Thank you for seeing it before I did. To my Grand Rapids coven of female artists: you are each magic, and our spells have only gotten stronger together. I'm so thankful to be nourished by each of your creative weaves in the world.

Lil Copan, you are the editor of my dreams, my final-hour Christmas miracle. Your sensitivity and masterful guidance gave me the courage to keep holding the chord of harmony in my own voice as a first-time author. Your embodied resonance allowed me to tune myself to the key of love through every page. Thank you.

To my manager, Jen Fodor, your belief in the midst of the daily grind is a tree trunk I lean on continually. Thank you for keeping me rooted and in believing in the multifaceted branches of my creativity without concern about the moreness of it all. Jonathan Merritt at Christopher Ferebee Agency, thank you for believing in and fighting for this project, for standing by the reframe of the erotic, and for seeing yourself in me and believing in this work as your own . . . and for the countless phone calls and the soul-mining mirroring at Chelsea Hotel.

I want to also acknowledge and thank each of the courageous students who took my seasonal creativity courses and who participated in the shaping of many of the lessons offered in these pages.

Last, I want to thank you, dear reader . . . for whatever small instinct you listened to that urged you to pick up this book. For the mysterious co-creative urge that led you to become woven together with me in this journey, I am so, so thankful. As I say to my kids when I tuck them in, I give you all my magic. Thank you for the gift of letting me give myself away to you in this way. We are all of us, always, becoming together, and the gift of this work is only made real by you receiving it. Thank you.

Notes

The Overture

vii ***Art is the act of triggering:*** David Whyte, from unknown source. Reprinted with permission from Many Rivers Press, Langley, WA, www.davidwhyte.com.

Making Love: An Introduction

xiii ***When I speak of the erotic:*** Audre Lorde, "Uses of the Erotic: The Erotic as Power" (paper delivered at the Fourth Berkshire Conference on the History of Women, Mount Holyoke College, MA, August 25, 1978). Published as a pamphlet by Out and Out Books (available from Crossing Press). Reprinted in Audre Lorde, *Sister Outsider: Essays and Speeches* (New York: Crossing Press, 1984), 55.

xxiii ***Context, good communication, and embodied presence to pleasurable sensation:*** Emily Nagoski, *Come as You Are* (New York: Simon & Schuster, 2021), 92.

Chapter One: Eros

10 ***Love is not a pleasant feeling***: Andreas Weber, *Matter and Desire: An Erotic Ecology* (originally published in German; Munich: Kosel Verlag, 2014; English ed., Chelsea Green Publishing, 2017), 8–9.

16 ***"I don't want to end up simply having visited"***: Mary Oliver, "When Death Comes," reprinted with permission of the Charlotte Sheedy Literary Agency as agent for the author. Copyright 1992, 2006, 2017 by Mary Oliver with permission of Bill Reichblum.

Chapter Two: Creative Chaos

20 ***Hesiod describes Eros as "a force of nature":*** Bruce S. Thornton, *Eros: The Myth of Ancient Greek Sexuality* (Boulder, CO: Westview Press, 1998), 13.

20 ***All things that represented upheaval:*** Thornton, *Eros*, 16.

21 ***Theologian and scholar Catherine Keller describes a harmonic relationship:*** Catherine Keller, *Face of the Deep: A Theology of Becoming* (New York: Routledge, 2003), 239.

21 ***One such story is the Pelagian myth of the goddess Eurynome:*** Keller, *Face of the Deep*, 14.

22 ***"The primal womb of the inappropriate":*** Bayo Akomolafe, *These Wilds beyond Our Fences: Letters to My Daughter on Humanity's Search for Home* (Berkley: North Atlantic Books, 2017), 128.

22 ***all monster myths are mother myths:*** Sophie Strand, *The Flowering Wand* (Rochester, VT: Inner Traditions, 2022), 23.

29 ***"The dark will be your home tonight":*** David Whyte, "Sweet Darkness," from *The House of Belonging*, Copyright 1997. Reprinted with permission from Many Rivers Press, Langley, WA. www.davidwhyte.com.

30 ***Eros is the "tyrant of the gods":*** Thornton, *Eros*, 13.

30 ***The desire to give up one world***: Cynthia Bourgeault, *The Meaning of Mary Magdalene* (Boston: Shambhala Press, 2010), 67.

30 ***"Only because of death does life become creative":*** Weber, *Matter and Desire*, 50.

Chapter Three: A Secret Seduction

35 ***Leaving one world with the aid of another:*** Bourgeault, *The Meaning of Mary Magdalene*, 67.

38 ***"Your image of God creates you":*** Richard Rohr, *Yes, and . . . : Daily Meditations* (Cincinnati: Franciscan Media, 2013, 2019), 65.

Chapter Four: (be)Coming Together

54 ***The body's way of knowing***: Akomolafe, *These Wilds beyond Our Fences*, 98.

54 ***According to Weber, the process is*** **enlivenment**: Weber, *Matter and Desire*, 16.

57 ***Bourgeault teaches what defines your personhood:*** Cynthia Bourgeault, "Teilhard Lecture on Personality and Personhood" (lecture, Living

School at the Center for Action and Contemplation, Albuquerque, NM, 2013–2015).

Chapter Five: ~~Good~~ Great Lovers

67 ***"If your daily life seems to lack material":*** Rainer Maria Rilke, *Letters to a Young Poet*, trans. Charlie Louth (London: Penguin Classics, 2011), chap. 1. Kindle.

68 ***"Gift exchange and erotic life are connected":*** Lewis Hyde, *The Gift: How the Creative Spirit Transforms the World* (New York: Vintage Books, 2019), chap. 1. Kindle.

70 ***"Domination is an asymmetrical, or nonreciprocal, relation":*** Beatrice Bruteau, *The Holy Thursday Revolution* (Maryknoll, NY: Orbis, 2005), 8.

70 ***"The domination paradigm pits self against the other":*** Bruteau, *Holy Thursday*, 27–28.

70 ***Bruteau describes it as a "symmetrical, reciprocal relation":*** Bruteau, *Holy Thursday*, 70.

71 ***"The drive to create," says Bruteau:*** Bruteau, *Holy Thursday*, 71.

73 ***It was a generous "I am":*** Bruteau, *Holy Thursday*, 71.

The Climax

79 ***"Maybe such devotion in which one holds the world":*** Mary Oliver, "Terms." Reprinted with permission of the Charlotte Sheedy Literary Agency as agent for the author. Copyright 2005, 2017 by Mary Oliver with permission of Bill Reichblum.

Chapter Seven: For(e) Play and Multiples

105 ***"[God] is . . . at the point of my pen":*** Pierre Teilhard de Chardin, *Hymn of the Universe*, trans. Simon Bartholomew (New York: Harper & Row, 1965), 84.

105 ***"still and still moving":*** T. S. Eliot, "East Coker," in *Four Quartets* (New York: Ecco Press, 2023), part 2. Kindle.

Chapter Eight: The Ache Is What Makes

111 ***Completion is not that goal; creativity is:*** Weber, *Matter and Desire*, 118.

114 ***"every separation is a link":*** Simone Weil, *Gravity and Grace* (New York: Putnam, 1952), 200.

Chapter Twelve: New Positions

159 ***"Creativity takes courage"***: Clint Brown, *Artist to Artist: Inspiration and Advise from Visual Artists Past and Present* (Peterborough, ON: Jackson Creek Press, 1998), chap. 12. Kindle.

Chapter Fourteen: Courageously Vulnerable

172 ***"The measure of our courage"***: David Whyte, "Disappointment," from *Consolations*. Copyright 2015. Reprinted with permission from Many Rivers Press, Langley, WA. www.davidwhyte.com.